CHOTHE GRAMMAR

CHOTHE GRAMMAR

By

Hidam Brojen Singh

AKANSHA PUBLISHING HOUSE
NEW DELHI-110002 (INDIA)

AKANSHA PUBLISHING HOUSE
4649-B/21, Ansari Road
Darya Ganj, New Delhi - 110 002
Ph.: 23263193 / 9811582579 / 09435116718
Fax: 011-23263193
Email: ektabooks@yahoo.com

Chothe Grammar

First Published 2008
ISBN 978-81-8370-143-3

PRINTED IN INDIA

Published by Akansha Publishing House, New Delhi and Printed at Aryan Enterprises, Delhi.

CONTENTS

FORWARD

There are more native speakers of Sino-Tibetan languages than any other language family in the world. In the Northeastern India, their are more than one hundred Tibeto-Berman (TB) languages which are not fully analysed. So, any analysis on any T.B. language in the North-east is very valuable: it is really a wealth to the Sino-Tibetanist. Dr. Hidam Brojen's book, called *"Chothe Grammar"*, I believed, will be appreciated by the Sino- Tebetanist specially. It is a descriptive grammar, having ten chapters. It includes phonology, roots and affixes, noun categories, verbal categories, word class, word formation, phrase and clauses, functional types of sentences and social grammar in which Dr. Brojen discusses the linguistics taboo in the Chothe society and terms of address. The last chapter shows how the native speakers use their language in the society. Dr. Brojen makes an attempt to describe the language fully: it is a good attempt. Hope he can go on exhaustive analysis in this language in the future.

Prof. **Chungkham Yashawanta Singh**
Department of Linguistics Manipur University

ACKNOWLEDGEMENT

As a linguist, I want to study the languages of Manipur which has 33 different indigenous mother tongues. For a quite long time the manuscript was lieying on my table, **"Chothe Grammar"**. Chothe is the one of the endangered languages of Manipur which is the Tibeto-Burman language family.

For this study, I get different helps from different persons as well as moral boost. I sincerely thank to Prof. Ch. Yashawanta Singh, M.U. for looking after me to solve any problem coming on my way. I also express my gratitude to Y. Maipak Chothe and Y. Tomal Chothe for helping my research work.

I am indebted to my colleagues, teachers and research persons for their moral support and encouragements. I sincerely dedicated to the Chothe Community of Manipur.

H. Brojen Singh

PREFACE

This book is the modification of my Ph.D. Thesis submitted to M.U. in December, 2000 entitled "A Descriptive Grammar of Chothe".

The book has ten chapters. The first chapter deals with Phonology. The Second Chapter discusses about Roots and Affixes. The third chapter deals with Noun categories about the gender, number, case, numerals, etc. The IV chapter deals with Verbal Categories. The V discusses about the Word Class i.e. nouns, pronouns, verbs, adjectives, adverbs, connectives, interjection etc. The VI chapter deals with Word Formation and Lexical rules. The chapter VII discusses about the Phrase and Clause. The VIII chapter deals with Syntactivization. The chapter IX discusses about Sentence Processes i.e. Declarative, Negation, Imperative and Interrogative sentences. The book also contents social grammar i.e. Taboo and Terms of Address in the chapter X. It has also Vocabularies and sample text in the appendix.

Hidam Brojen Singh

INTRODUCTION

From the legend, **Chothe** tribe was derived from the name of the first man **Kachokte** who was blessed by god **Pakhangpa** viz, **Kachokte>Chokte>Chote>Chothe**. Grierson (1904) wrote "Chote" in the Linguistic Survey of India, Vol III,Part III, page 262. Chothe belongs to old Kuki sub-group of Kuki-Chin of Tibeto-Burman Language family of the Sino-Tibetan group.

From time immemorial, the people of Chothe believed that they came out from a cave known **"Huipithoranga"** i. e. **huipi** "cave" and **thoranga** "five shibs". The cave was covered by a flat rock. In course of time, the cave was opened by a monkey. After the cave was opened the Chothe men and women came out on the earth's surface and settled there many years. In course of time a son and a daughter were born to them. The god **Pakhangpa** directed them to name the children as **Kachokte** and **Thanidam** respectively. After that, almost all the Chothe men and women were eaten up by **Kamkayrangpa** "tiger" except the two children **Kachokte** and **Thanidam** who were carefully guarded by god **Pakhangpa** against wild beasts. By the bleassing of god **Pakhangpa**, **Kachokte** and **Thanidam** were born five sons and two daughters. They lived many years at **Huipithoranga**. Due to increase in population they made their village administration rules. After sometimes, they migrated many villages from **Huipithoranga.**

Chothe tribes are mainly inhabited in the Bishnupur and Chandel district. The total Chothe villages are seventeen only in Manipur. Out of these seventeen; fifteen villages are situated in Chandel district and the remaining two villages are situated in Bishnupur district. The names of Chothe villages of the Chandel district are:- (i) Tampakhu (ii) Laininghu (iii) Chumbang (iv) Khongkhang (v) Ajouhu (vi) Phantu (vii) Chothe hunou (Lamlanglon) (viii) Chandonpokpi (ix) Ziontlang (x) Salemthar (xi)Lirungtabi (xii) Lunghu (xiii) Lungleh (xiv) Old Wangparal and (xv) New Wangparal. The chothe villages, namely; (i) Lamlanghupi and (ii) Lamlanglon are situated in Bishnupur district.

The Chothe possess a distinct identity with reference to other tribe of Manipur and is one of the oldest tribe in Manipur because they arrived in Bishnupur area (Manipur) from the time immemorial. Due to increase in population, some Chothe tribes are migrated to the Chandel district.

Originally, Chothe tribe had only five sibs viz; (i) Kheyang/ Khiyang (ii) Yuhlung (iii) Makan (iv) Marim and (v) Thao. Later on it increased to seven sibs. The present structure of sub-sibs from the original sibs may be summarized as follows according to the seven patrilineal exogamy in Chothe society. They are as follows:-

(i) Kheyang/Khiyang with four sub-sibs, namely, Inpi, Inte, Aihung and Lungkung.
(ii) Yuhlung with one sub-sib, i. e. Tangkim.
(iii) Makan with three sub-sibs, namely, Kankung, Makante and Lasik.
(iv) Marim with four sub-sibs, which are, Rimphunchong, Rimkung, Rimke-lek and Pilling.
(v) Thao with two sub-sibs, which are Thaokung and Thaorun.
(vi) Parpa without any sub-sib.
(vii) Rangsi with one sub-sib, namely, Teyu.

Chothe marriage system is strictly observed in the patrilineal exogamy. Inter-sib marriage is strictly followed while intra-sib marriage is generally prohibited. Marriage within the sub-sib is also strictly prohibited according to Chothe marriage system. Polygamy is allowed in the Chothe society but seldom practiced.

Divorce is theoretically allowed but practically negligible. Marriage of widow or widower is also allowed in the Chothe customs.

Agriculture is the main occupation of the Chothe. The main agriculture products are rice, maize, arum, banana, potato, sweet potato etc. They eat rice with vegetable, fish and meat. They formerly practised shifting cultivation. Now most of people have shifted to wet cultivation.

Houses of the Chothe are constructed with wood and bamboo on the ground. Men is their leisure time make baskets, fishing net or do carpentry work or catch fish etc., while women weave cloths and prepare liquor. Traditionally they like tight dresses. Necklace, earrings, bangles are used by their members. They had many patterns of dresses made by cotton. The people have a brown complexion, black hair and the eye of classical mongoloid type. They are good natured and trustworthy. They enjoy a peaceful life and are full of hospitality. The whole community of Chothe is administered by the traditional village council under a Hulakpa, Head of the village.

Hunting, fighting, devotion to god and goddess, singing and dancing, blacksmith, animal husbandry and games and sports are also practiced in their social life.

The data of this work is collected from Lamlanghupi and Lamlanglong village, about 35 Km from Imphal situated in Bishnupur district which is the oldest village in Manipur (Standhop Yunglung, 1986). The informants are Y. Maipak Chothe, Y. Tomal chothe, Kh. Thambaljao Chothe and Kh. Dimho Chothe.

It is a descriptive Grammar of Chothe. It makes an attempt to describe the language from the speech sound system to the sentence level.

ABBREVIATION

WORDS

Accusative	acc.
Adverbial marker	adv.mk
Adverb phrase	Ad.P.
Affectionate	aff
Archaic	arc.
Associative	asso
Attributive	att.
Beneficiary	ben.
Command marker	com.mk.
Complete	comp.
Confirmative	conf.
Continuous aspect	CON.asp.
Co-ordinate	Corn.
Copula	cop.
Definite	def.
Delimitative	del.
Determiner	det.
Distance determiner	ddet.
Distributive	dis.
Exclusive	exc
Emphatic	emph.
Female	F
Formative particle	F.P.
Future marker	f.mk.
Genitive	gen.
Honorific marker	HON.mk.

Inclusive	incl.
Infinitive	inf.
Instrumental	inst.
Locative	loc.
Male	M
Negative	neg.
Nominalizer	NZ.
Nominative	nom.
Noun phrase	NP
Ordinal marker	ord.mk.
Particle	part.
Peremptory	perem.
Perfective aspect	PER.asp.
Plural	pl.
Potential	pot.
Pronominal prefix	pp
Proposal marker	prop.mk.
Proximal determiner	pdet
Question marker	Q.mk.
Reciprocal	rec.
Reflexive	ref.
Sentence particle	SP.
Singular	Sg.
Unrealized aspect	UNR.asp.
Verb	V.
Verb phrase	VP.
Vocative	voc.

SIGN

~	allomorph
>	becomes
=	equal
`	falling tone
*	ungrammatical
ø	zero morph

ONE

PHONOLOGY

Chothe has 29 phonemes. They are divided into segmental and suprasegmental phonemes. Segmental phonemes are 6 vowels and 21 consonants. Suprasegmental phonemes are 2 tones, that is, level tone and falling tone. They are discussed in the following relevant sections.

Vowels

The six vowel phonemes are divided into three according to the height of the tongue as high, mid and low. They are shown in the table1.

Chart of the vowel phonemes

	Front		Central		Back	
	Rounded	Un-Rounded	Rounded	Un-Rounded	Rounded	Un-Rounded
High		i			u	
Mid		e		ə	o	
Low				a		

Table1

Articulatory description of these six vowels are given below:-

i- High, front, unrounded vowel

e- Mid, front, unrounded vowel

ə- Mid, central, unrounded vowel

a- Low, central, unrounded vowel

u- High, back, rounded vowel

o- Mid, back, rounded vowel

These six vowels are established on the basis of the following minimal pairs.

i/e	:	in	'drink'
		en	'bitten by animal'
ə/a	:	səŋ	'spear'
		saŋ	'paddy'
o/u	:	om	'save'
		um	'gourd'

Some other minimal pairs are given below:-

i/a	:	in	'drink'
		an	'look upward'
i/u	:	pin	'border/lace'
		pun	'cloth'
i/o	:	lik	'louse'
		lok	'big'
e/u	:	lek	'slice of bamboo'
		luk	'harvest'
e/o	:	ek	'dung'
		ok	'pig'
ə/a	:	ləm	'land'
		lam	'dance'
a/e	:	ak	'crow'
		ek	'dung'

a/u	:	haŋ	'black'
		huŋ	'mridanga'
a/o	:	sa	'sing'
		so	'lock'
o/u	:	om	'save'
		um	'gourd'

Dristribution of vowels

All the six vowels can occur initially, medially and finally. Their distributions are discussed in the following:-

Initial Occurrence

/i/	in	'drink'
	incuŋ	'roof'
	inhak	'surname'
	inhakpi	'wall lizard'
/e/	e	'do'
	ek	'dung'
	en	'bitten by animal'
	ekmuy	'beetle'
/ə/	ən	'look'
	əbu	'leaf'
	əco	'pillar'
	əju	'rate'
/a/	ak	'crow'
	an	'look upward'
	am	'design structure of cloth'
/u/	uni	'today'
	uŋa	'child'
	um	'gourd'
	usəkte	'sparrow'
/o/	on	'belly'
	okt^{h}u	'wild boar'

	onkiya	'colic pain'
	onna-a	'belly pain'

Medial Occurrence

/i/	lik	'louse'
	tiŋ	'nail'
	kin	'his time'
	t^him	'box'
/e/	cet	'tight'
	lek	'slice bamboo'
	heŋ	'tub'
	seŋ	'dress up'
/ə/	səŋ	'spear'
	cəŋ	'right'
	ləm	'land'
	dəŋ	'know'
/a/	saŋ	'paddy'
	haŋ	'black'
	taŋ	'chest'
	caŋ	'net'
/u/	pum	'health'
	tuk	'meet'
	luk	'harvest'
	sum	'mortar'
/o/	kot	'door'
	koŋ	'waist'
	hoŋ	'neck'
	lok	'big'

Final Occurrence

/i/	si	'cow'
	ci	'salt'
	li	'say'
	hi	'bull fight'

/e/	be	'pot'
	ke	'leg'
	he	'pare'
	ne	'able'
/ə/	t^hebə	'rabbit'
	hukpə	'to beat'
	dikpə	'fresh'
	bəkpə	'to eat'
/a/	ha	'teeth'
	ba	'slip'
	na	'banana leaf'
	ta	'binding bamboo'
/u/	bu	'rice'
	lu	'head'
	hu	'village'
	ju	'liquor'
/o/	so	'lock'
	p^ho	'shield'
	do	'request for share'
	ho	'to prick with a spear'

Vowel Sequence.

Vowel phonemes come one after another in disyllabic and trisyllabic words are known as vowel sequence. In Chothe, the vowel **i** can occur with the vowels **e** and ə, vowel ə can occur with the six vowels, vowel **a** can occur only the vowel **a** and vowel **u** can occur with the vowels **i** and ə in the vowel sequence. Few examples are given in the following:-

si-ek	'cow dung'
səki-ətə	'fawn'
lə-i	'line'
kə-ek	'my dung'
kə-ən	'my curry'
kə-ok	'my pig'

kə-am 'my design structure of cloth'
kə-u 'sister-in-law'
onna-a 'belly pain'
ləyhu-in 'temple'
əsu-əroməmləwpə 'infinite'

Consonants

Chothe has twentyone consonant phonemes. These consonants can represent on the point or place of articulation and the manner of articulation which are set out horizontally and vertically respectively. These consonant phonemes make distinction between aspirated and unaspirated especially for stop. It has distinction between stop, fricatives, nasal, flap/tap, lateral, approximant etc. The consonant phonemes primarily show in six positions, namely, bilabial, alveolar, palatal, velar, labial velar and glottal in the categories of voiced and voiceless (see table II).These twentyone consonant can be established on the basis of the following minimal pairs or overlapping words. The following examples denote a contrast between the two consonants.

Examples:-

p/b	:	pe	'give'
		be	'pot'
t/d	:	ta	'bamboo slice'
		da	'rotten egg'
k/g	:	kot	'door'
		got	'court'
		kom	'edge of basket'
		gom	'gum'
b^h/t^h		b^hu	'plate'
		t^hu	'shake'
t^h/p^h	:	t^hi	'die'
		p^hi	'twin'
		t^ho	'presentation'
		p^ho	'shield'

k/k^h	:	kuŋ	'boat"
		k^{h}uŋ	'top'
		kay	'pull(grain)'
		k^{h}ay	'seperate'
t/t^h	:	tum	'step down'
		t^{h}um	'sweet'
		to	'footing on'
		t^{h}o	'presentation'
m/ŋ	:	mi	'man'
		ŋi	'stand'
		om	'save'
		oŋ	'sit'
n/l	:	nəy	'lip'
		ləy	'flower'
		nok	'shake (tree)'
		lok	'big'
r/l	:	re	'return'
		le	'speak'
		ru	'rain'
		lu	'head'
s/h	:	sa	'sing'
		ha	'teeth'
		soŋ	'worship'
		hoŋ	'neck'
d/l	:	di	'like'
		li	'say'
		day	'calm'
		lay	'war'
b/c	:	bi	'hide'
		ci	'salt'
		ba	'slip'
		ca	'hate'

y/j	:	yun	'urine'
		jun	'throw'
		yəm	'coward'
		jəm	'spread'
w/y	:	waŋ	'tall'
		yaŋ	'lightness'
		əwa	'bird'
		əya	'elder brother'

Consonant Phonemes

		Bilabial		Alveolar		Palatal		Labial velar		Velar		Glottal	
		Vd.-less	Vd.	Vd.-less	Vd.	Vd.-less	Vd.	Vd.-less	Vd.	Vd.-less	Vd.	Vd.-less	Vd.
Stop	Unaspirated	p	b	t	d	c	j			k	g		
	Aspirated	p^h	b^h	t^h						k^h			
Nasal			m		n						ŋ		
Fricative						s						h	
Flap/tap					r								
Lateral					l								
Approximant							y		w				

Table II

Distribution of Consonants

Initial Occurrence of Consonants:-

p	:	pun	'cloth'
		pum	'health'
		pəŋ	'a rack'
		paywa	'swan'
b	:	butoy	'bread'
		buyhu	'cold'
		basəw	'soyabean'
		betak	'chick'
t	:	tay	'basket'

		toŋ	'language'
		tuy	'water'
		tuypute	'king fisher'
d	:	donpə	'plenty'
		daypə	'old'
		dumde	'glow-worm'
		deropə	'bright'
c	:	cəm	'dagger'
		cisay	'rice'
		ceklaŋ	'dragon fly'
		ceŋkʰa	'bitter gourd'
j	:	jappə	'to blow'
		jəmpə	'coward'
		jiŋtiŋ	'night'
		jurite	'squirrel'
k	:	kot	'door'
		kekok	'shoe'
		kaŋkrawpi	'cockroach'
		kəpotʰəy	'promegranate'
g	:	got	'court'
		gom	'gum'
bʰ	:	bʰu	'plate'
		bʰeləndri	'ladysfinger'
pʰ	:	pʰurupte	'moth'
		pʰəyboy	'nightingale'
		pʰuyraŋ	'a bird'
		pʰəyjoy	'flat-land'
tʰ	:	tʰiŋto	'tree'
		tʰiŋraŋ	'air'
		tʰiŋna	'grass'
		tʰəytup	'apple'

k^h	:	k^haŋ	'flying pan'
		k^hutp^{h}a	'palm'
		k^hutsəbik	'ring'
		k^həcakpə	'bitter'
m	:	mun	'pillow'
		mənto	'brinjal'
		mənsu	'sugarcane'
		muyron	'hill'
n	:	na	'banana leaf'
		na-a	'patient'
		nem	'soft'
		nərəŋ	'page'
ŋ	:	ŋipə	'to stand'
		ŋəypa	'leopard'
		ŋəycat	'wasp'
		ŋaruy	'eel fish'
r	:	re	'return'
		rəha	'chin'
		reŋnu	'queen'
		rəŋa	'five'
l	:	la	'thread'
		luwa	'vomiting'
		ləyt^{h}a	'white ant'
		liŋlut	'shirt'
s	:	sora	'lion'
		səy	'spear'
		səŋŋi	'ant'
		sihom	'milk'
h	:	hatəy	'ladle'
		hupa	'cough'
		huymu	'black bee'
		haŋŋəy	'mosquito net'

y	:	yoŋ	'search'
		yun	'urine'
		yuŋ	'fly'
		yəytim	'taro'
w	:	wa	'come'
		wan	'Jully'
		woy	'left'
		wansaŋ	'table'

Medial Occurrence

All the consonant phonemes can occur in the intervocalic position except the consonant **g** in the words as exemplified below:-

p	:	lapon	'sheep'
		cipot	'a gourd'
		hupə	'cough'
		yupi	'coconut'
b	:	əbu	'leaf'
		əbe	'bean'
		əbo	'November'
		əbay	'book'
t	:	butoy	'bread'
		nitak	'west'
		site	'calf'
		ətu	'spade'
d	:	lude	'bold'
		ludoypə	'idle'
		ədəŋ	'other'
c	:	əco	'pillar'
		ucum	'dove'
		əcay	'dry'
		əcom	'punch'
j	:	əja	'itching'
		əju	'rate'

		əjuŋ	'seed'
		əjoŋ	'monkey'
k	:	səkoy	'horse'
		kukaŋ	'bed'
		məku	'owl'
		nukuy	'ear'
p^h	:	$əp^həy$	'market'
		$səp^ha$	'procupine'
		$əp^hi$	'twin'
		$əp^ha$	'time'
t^h	:	$ət^ha$	'wing'
		lut^huk	'brain'
		$ət^həy$	'habit'
		$ət^hum$	'sugar'
k^h	:	$ək^ha$	'one'
		$tək^həy$	'selbum'
		$ək^hutiŋ$	'elbow'
		$ək^hakum$	'and'
m	:	əmuy	'feather'
		əmay	'pumkin'
		tumay	'courtyard'
		puma	'abcess'
n	:	ənoy	'pig'
		ənəw	'champa'
		hinake	'here'
		sənəkuŋ	'tortoise'
ŋ	:	ləŋi	'thatch'
		əŋəm	'duty'
		siŋetpə	'to care'
r	:	sirim	'mitten'
		siroy	'buffalo'
		əruy	'snake'
		peroŋ	'reed'

l	:	ciləm	'condition'
		haləw	'May'
		ilupə	'to steal'
s	:	əsat	'bug'
		məsi	'pepper'
		basəw	'soyabean'
		cisay	'rice'
h	:	buhu	'a shallow basket'
		kehap	'step'
		rəha	'chin'
		lahaŋ	'chair'
w	:	əwa	'bird'
		luwa	'vomiting'
		t^həway	'shadow'
		suway	'husk'
y	:	leyə	'request'
		heyə	'more'
		məyek	'charcoal'
		p^hiyuŋ	'bloom'

Final Occurrence

Of the twenty consonant phonemes, only ten consonant phonemes can occur in the final position of words in Chothe. They are **p,t,k,m,n,ŋ,r,l,w** and **y** as exemplified below:-

p	:	dop	'hip'
		əprep	'piece'
		ətip	'day after tomorrow'
		p^hurup	'butterfly'
		kəŋkuycep	'burning beetle'
t	:	kot	'door'
		əsat	'bug'
		əmot	'banana'
		liŋlut	'shirt'
		ŋaycat	'wasp'

k	:	lik	'louse'
		əpek	'wide'
		aytok	'duck'
		luysok	'cobra'
		əmətok	'comb'
m	:	ucum	'dove'
		dum	'duty'
		pum	'health'
		gom	'gum'
		nem	'soft'
n	:	pin	'lace'
		min	'ripe'
		wan	'Jully'
		won	'belly'
		lapon	'sheep'
ŋ	:	teŋ	'wash'
		koŋ	'waist'
		caŋ	'net'
		kuŋ	'boat'
		luŋ	'heart'
r	:	cinar	'melon'
		toŋŋir	'decide'
l	:	sirkal	'September'
		yupal	'a designation of ruling'
		ləwkol	'ruling bench'
		taytel	'a trellis used for sitting'
w	:	ləw	'medicine'
		səw	'buble'
		haw	'locust'
		sərəw	'oath'
		piŋpreəw	'swallow'
y	:	koy	'bracelet'
		muy	'mouth'

nay	'near'
lay	'war'
səy	'spear'

Consonant Clusters

It is the occurrence of two consonants within a syllable. The system of the consonant clusters of the Tibeto-Burman languages are of two types:- (a) stop or nasal + liquid (**r~l**), (b) consonant (or cluster of foregoing type) + semi vowel (**w~y**) (Benedict, 1972). The two types of consonant clusters are found in Aimol (Shamungou, 1995). But in the case of Chothe, the consonant cluster is only one type i. e. stop + liquid. The consonat cluster of Chothe is rarely found in the medial position of the word as given below:-

Stop + liquid

kr-	t^hiŋ-kripə	'clear'
	koŋ-krik	'grass hopper'
	kəŋ-krawpi	'cockroach'
br-	mi-brəy	'tip of tongue'
pr-	piŋ-preəw	'swallow'
tr-	koŋ-truk	'snipe'
	tiŋ-triknu	'witch'

Sequence of Consonants

When two or more consonants are occurred in an immediate position, beyond the syllable it is regarded as consonant sequence. A number of consonants can have immediate occurrence as given in the following examples:-

p : can occur with the consonants **p, k^h, n,** and **h** only.

p + p	hup-pə	'to bind'
	jap-pə	'to blow'
p + k^h	nəp-k^hi	'crust'
p + n	pop-nopə	'blunt'
p + h	t^hep-hoŋpə	'folding of cloth'

t : can have an immediate occurrence with **p,t,c,j,k,pʰ,tʰ,m,n,l,s,**and **h.**

t + p	əwet-pə	'mad'
	mit-pə	'extinguish'
t + t	kot-te	'window'
	mit-tuy	'tear'
t + c	mit-cowa	'blind'
t + j	kʰut-jay	'iron finger'
t + k	mit-kuy	'eye brow'
	əmot-ki	'date palm'
t + pʰ	kʰut-pʰa	'palm'
t + tʰ	pʰit-tʰakpə	'to fight'
t + m	mit-muy	'eye lash'
t + n	əkʰut-niŋ	'elbow'
t + l	but-ləwpə	'raw'
t + s	əhut-soŋ	'gun'
t + h	mit-həw	'eye lid'
	kʰut-hoŋ	'joint of hand'

k : can occur with **p,b,t,d,c,k,pʰ, tʰ,m,n,l,**and **s.**

k + p	dik-pə	'green'
	hok-pu	'knee'
k + b	tək-buywa	'bath'
k + t	sak-tiŋ	'north'
	usək-te	'sparrow'
k + d	jik-dot	'script'
k + c	sək-cak	'food'
	lok-cokpə	'proud'

k + k	t^hək-ka	'elergy'
	tarok-ka	'ulcer'
k + p^h	tuybak-p^həm	'port'
k + t^h	lik-t^ha	'tick'
	ok-t^hu	'wild boar'
k + m	ek-muy	'beetle'
	ok-me	'pork'
k + n	lok-nu	'pigeon'
	nisuk-na	'dawn'
k + l	tək-la	'wart'
	cek-laŋ	'dragonfly'
k + s	suk-soy	'snail'
	əruk-sa	'empty'

m : can occur with the consonant **p,t,d,c,j,k,p^h, t^h,m,n,r,l,s,h** and **w**.

m + p	jəm-pə	'coward'
	t^him-pi	'mid-wife'
m + t	cəm-te	'knife'
m + d	dum-de	'glow-worm'
m + c	ləm-cəm	'sword'
	əŋəm-ciya	'busy'
m + j	sim-joy	'monkey'
	əjəm-ja	'a part (seperation of heart and lungs)'
m + k	ləm-koypə	'travel'
m + p^h	tim-p^ha	'leech'
	sum-p^hay	'cloud'
m + t^h	kum-t^həw	'January'
	t^him-t^huy	'box'

m + m	ləm-mu	'kite'
	dom-ma	'thank'
m + n	əm-nopə	'tire'
	ləysem-ni	'Tuesday'
m + r	ləm-rapə	'distance'
m + l	sim-ləy	'earth'
	pum-li	'breast'
m + s	pum-suka	'swelling'
	əpum-sapə	'fat'
m + h	t^{h}em-hoŋpə	'console'
	p^{h}əm-hoŋpə	'freeze'
m + w	cəm-watta	'operation'

n : can occur with **p,b,t,d,c,j,k,p^h,t^h,k^h,n,l,s,h** and **w.**

n + p	men-pə	'to catch'
	lon-pə	'to carry'
n + b	ən-be	'curry pot'
n + t	ən-təm	'mustard'
	mən-to	'brinjal'
n + d	pun-duŋŋa	'curtain'
	ən-doyən-dapə	'enemy'
n + c	sən-coŋba	'purple'
	ulin-cəŋpa	'elder'
n + j	ənjon-pə	'nice'
n + k	un-koy	'skin'
	on-kiya	'colic pain'
n + p^h	pun-p^{h}a	'bed sheet'
	t^{h}an-p^{h}əm	'grave'
n + t^h	t^{h}ən-t^{h}akpə	'divorce'
	ətun-t^{h}əwwa	'influenza'

n + k^h	cipən-k^ha	'fort'
n + n	ən-no	'reed'
	ətun-na	'now'
n + l	in-lupə	'thief'
	sən-ləwpa	'yellow'
n + s	mən-su	'surgarcane'
	wan-saŋ	'tumbler'
n + h	pun-hu	'quilt'
	in-hakpi	'wall lizard'
n + w	lon-wapə	'to bring'

ŋ : can occur with the consonant phonemes
p,b,t,c,j,k,p^h,t^h,k^h, m,n,ŋ,l,s,h,and **w**.

ŋ + p	toŋ-pi	'friend'
	saŋ-pəŋ	'granary store'
ŋ + b	cəŋ-ban	'hand'
	səncoŋ-pa	'purple'
ŋ + t	suŋ-tu	'typhoid'
	ləŋ-tiya	'vulture'
ŋ + d	həyiŋ-dəŋ	'down'
ŋ + c	luŋ-cəlhoypə	'gentle'
	əwat^{h}iŋ-cupi	'wood peaker'
ŋ + j	luŋ-jube	'jar'
	məraŋ-jay	'town'
ŋ + k	koŋ-kəp	'oyster'
	laŋ-kon	'float'
ŋ + p^h	saŋ-p^hun	'April'
	t^hiraŋ-p^həybu	'gale'
ŋ + t^h	təŋ-t^han	'mosquito'
	suŋ-t^huy	'cholera'

ŋ + k^h	ceŋ-k^ha	'bitter gourd'
	əŋ-k^hapə	'equal'
ŋ + m	cuŋ-məcay	'worm cast'
ŋ + n	luŋ-ni	'day'
	reŋ-nu	'queen'
ŋ + ŋ	səŋ-ŋəy	'wolf'
	toŋ-ŋir	'decide'
ŋ + l	liŋ-lut	'shirt'
	cəŋ-loŋ	'banana tree'
ŋ + s	piŋ-sən	'piles'
	toŋ-sukno	'dump'
ŋ + h	səŋ-him	'chicken pox'
	luŋ-he	'lungs'
ŋ + w	t^haŋ-wan	'space'

r : can have an immediate occurrence with **p,k,m** and **h**.

r + p	pər-pa	'a clan of Chothe'
r + k	sir-kal	'September'
r + m	p^hur-muy	'dogs of all kinds'
r + h	ər-ha	'chin'

l : can make a consonant sequence with the phonemes **l** and **h** only.

l+l	sel-lebay	'cousin (brother)'
	ol-la	'sorrow'
l + h	luŋcəl-hoypa	'gentle'

y : can occur with the consonants **p,b,t,d,c,j,k,p^h,t^h,k^h,m,n, ŋ,r, l,s,h,w** and **y**.

y + p	səy-pi	'elephant'
	kəy-pə	'to shut'

y + b	huy-bu	'hive'
	p^həy-bi	'winter'
y + t	huy-tuy	'honey'
	yəy-tim	'taro'
y + d	ləy-don	'debt'
	p^həy-dəŋ	'bow'
y + c	əy-ci	'star'
	ay- caŋ	'peacock'
y + j	p^həy-joy	'valley'
	səy-juy	'step sister'
y + k	ay-kiŋ	'lizard'
	hoy-ke	'where'
y + p^h	ay-p^huyri	'garlic'
	tuy-p^huy	'foam'
y + t^h	luy-t^həy	'youth'
	əy-t^hiŋ	'ginger'
y + k^h	t^həy-k^ha	'plum'
	p^həy-k^hapə	'fencing'
y + m	ay-me	'chicken'
	say-məy	'fire (arc.)'
y + n	ərəy-na	'disease'
	numəy-nu	'woman'
y + ŋ	ləy-ŋuy	'sand'
y + r	buy-rəy	'dress'
	t^həy-ru	'arrow'
y + l	tuy-laymi	'navy'
	ənt^{h}uy-luy	'jute'
y + s	way-si	'parasol'
	nukuy-set	'deaf'

y + h	ləy-huy	'cave'
	ləy-hu	'god'
y + w	pəy-wa	'goose'
	coy-wapə	'to carry'
y + y	hoy-yə	'mourn'
	liŋləy-yə	'gift'

w : can have an immediate accurrence with **p,t,k,t^{h},m,n,ŋ,r,h,w** and **y**.

w + p	t^{h}arəw-pə	'evil'
	naw-poŋ	'younger'
w + t	ut^{h}əw-te	'hawk'
	həw-toŋ	'cat'
w + k	jəw-kun	'garden'
	ləw-kəl	'ruling bench'
w + t^{h}	t^{h}əw-t^{h}uk	'event'
	asaw-t^{h}a	'summer'
w + m	ləw-muy	'field'
	ləw-mu	'tablet'
w + n	kəw-nu	'sister'
	ət^{h}əw-na	'origin'
w + ŋ	unaw-ŋəy	'half brother'
w + r	t^{h}əyt^{h}aməw-riya	'wedding'
w + h	t^{h}əw-huy	'honey bee'
	nəw-huŋna	'cradle'
w + w	saykaw-wa	'curse'
	pumt^{h}əw-wa	'swelling'
w + y	əw-yetpə	'sad'

Diphthong-like Sound

Chothe has no pure diphthong. When an approximant occurs

after the vowel, a diphthong-like sound is created. Some examples are given in the following:-

əw	əwpə	'shout'
	ləw	'medicine'
əy	əysi	'star'
	səy	'spear'
	hatəy	'laddle'
aw	awpə	'a long step'
	haw	'locust'
	paw	'pile up'
ay	aytok	'duck'
	əbay	'book'
	əray	'naval'
oy	oypə	'sorrow'
	toy	'thigh'
	koy	'bracelet'
uy	uy	'dog
	uytok	'toad'
	nukuy	'ear'

Syllable

The syllable is a unit of pronunciation consisting of a vowel alone or of a vowel with one or more consonants. A vowel is the nucleus and consonant a marginal element in the syllable, that is, a consonant either at the beginning or at the end of a syllable. "Tibeto-Burman languages are generally portrayed as isolating, 'monosyllabic' languages in which words are classified according to syntactic funtion rather than according to the affixes than can or must occur" (Hale, 1982).

Structure of syllables

The vowel or diphthong is the nucleus or peak of the syllable. The consonant (or consonants) before the peak is called onset and the consonant (or consonants) after the peak is called coda.

For instance:-

pun 'cloth'
- Code
- Peak
- Omset

If the syllable end in a vowel, it is called an open syllable; if it ends in a consonant, it is a closed syllable.

Open syllables		Closed syllables	
si	'cow'	in	'house'
ha	'teeth'	ek	'dung'
be	'pot'	ən	'curry'
hu	'village'	on	'belly'

Syllabic Pattern

On the basis of occurrence of vowel (V) and consonant (C), the syllabic pattern can be divided into five in Chothe. They are given below:-

I	V	ì	'what'
		e	'do'
		u	'frog'
II	VC	in	'drink'
		ak	'crow'
		om	'save'
III	CV	ci	'salt'
		lu	'head'
		ke	'leg'
IV	CVC	lik	'louse'
		kot	'door'
		pum	'health'
V	CCVC	brəy	'tongue'
		bray	'winnowing fan'

Syllabic Division

V-CV	ə-be	'bean'
	ə-tu	'spads
	ə-ca	'wax'
V-CVC	ə-tun	'fever'
	ə-kəm	'chapter'
	u-cum	'dove'
V-CCV	ə-tra	'sound'
VC-CV	ok-me	'pork'
	əy-ci	'star'
	əw-pə	'shout'
VC-CVC	ek-muy	'beetle'
	ən-təm	'mustard'
	ən-nim	'onion'
CV-V	lə-i	'line'
	kə-u	'sister-in-law'
CV-VC	si-ek	'cowdung'
	kə-ok	'my pig'
CV-CV	ju-be	'wine pot'
	mə-si	'pepper'
	mə-ku	'owl'
CV-CVC	bu-toy	'bread'
	be-tak	'chick'
CV-CCVC	mi-brəy	'tip of tongue'
CVC-CV	pəy-wa	'goose'
	pun-hu	'quilt'
	dom-ma	'thank'
CVC-CVC	luy-tum	'cobra'
	way-noy	'flour'
	lok-cok	'proud'

CVC-CCVC	kaŋ-truk	'snipe'
	koŋ-krik	'grass hopper'

Syllabification:

Syllables can also be classified into monosyllabic, disyllabic and polysyllabic words. Examples are given below:-

Monosyllabic words:-

in	'drink'
hoŋ	'neck'
dop	'hip'
pun	'cloth'

Disyllabic words:-

so-ra	'lion'
li-kok	'glass'
yu-hom	'bottle'
lu-tuk	'brain'

Polysyllabic words:-

kə-po-tʰəy	'promegranate'
sə-koy-pu-nu	'mare'
luŋ-lut-la-ni-pə	'zeal'
ə-suŋ-toŋ-way-si-pa	'conspire'
tʰəy-ra-luŋ-la-ə-rik-te	'grain'
tʰəy-ra-luŋ-la-ə-rik-te-ŋəy	'grains'

Tone

As a Tibeto-Burman language, Chothe has the tonal system in the sense that pitch variation affects the meaning of the word by level or by falling etc. " When a syllable is associated with a particular pitch level such as high, mid, low etc., and the pitch distinguishes the meanings of words, then the pitch is called tone and the language which has tone is a tone language.Tone is a feature of the lexicon, being described in terms of prescribed pitches for syllables or sequences of pitches for morphemes or words", (Clark and Yallop, 1990).

There are two tones in Chothe, namely, (a) level tone and (b) falling tone (level tone is not marked here and falling tone is marked as '`'). But in the case of Chinese and Ao Naga, it has three tones. Meiteron (Manipuri), Punjabi and Koireng have two tones. These two tones can be established by the minimal pairs as given below:-

Level tones		Falling tones	
la	'thread'	là	'song'
ci	'salt'	cì	'spittle'
in	'drink'	ìn	'house'
kum	'also'	kùm	'age'
um	'gourd'	ùm	'yes'
muy	'mouth'	mùy	'body hair'
tay	'dalay'	tày	'demand'
haw	'bag'	hàw	'locust'
ay	'hen'	ày	'crab'

TWO

ROOT AND AFFIXES

Root

A root is a form which is not further analyzable either in terms of derivational or inflectional morphology. A root is the basic part always present in a lexeme. The root can be classified into two types i.e. free root and bound root.

In this language, the free root can be found in monosyllabic, disyllabic and polysyllabic words. It may be divided into Nominal free roots and Verbal Free roots.

Nominal Free roots

(a) Monosyllabic free roots

ok 'pig'
ek 'dung'
be 'pot'
si 'cow'
lik 'louse'
lam 'dance'

(b) Disyllabic free roors

bu-toy 'bread'
luy-tum 'cobra'
li-kok 'glass'
be-tak 'chick'
nu-kuy 'ear'
way-si 'parasol'

(c) Polysyllabic free roots

bə-rəy-tun	'guava'
bu-bi-tay	'hamper'
tuy-pu-te	'king fisher'
do-yəy-tʰə-nu	'witch'
moy-mə-raŋ-caŋ	'spider'
tʰəy-ra-luŋ-ia-ə-rik-te	'grain'

Verbal free roots

(a) Monosyllabic free roots

in	'drink'
pe	'give'
teŋ	'wash'
tʰəw	'fly'
pʰuy	'cut'
huk	'beat' , etc.

(b) Disyllabic free roots

tə-pən	'kick'
toŋ-ŋir	'decide'
tuŋ-tʰak	'meet'
tuy-hoŋ	'combine'
dom-ma	'thank'
nay-suk	'escape', etc.

(c) Polysyllabic free roots

su-hoŋ-tʰak	'collide'
ə-ti-ya-nok	'tremble'
ə-tʰuy-doy	'depend'
mək-pi-ne	'quench'
toŋ-tʰin-na	'praise', etc.

Bound roots

In Chothe, kinship terms are bound roots as exemplified below:-

-pa	'father'
-nu	'mother'

-nute 'aunt'
-upa 'elder brother'
-nawpa 'younger brother', etc.

Until and unless one of the personal pronouns **kə-** 'first person', **nə-** 'second person' and **mə-** 'third person' are added ; it does not give a complete meaning, for instances; **kəpa** 'my father',**nəpa** 'your father', **məpa** 'his father', etc.

Affixes:-

Affixes are bound roots which can only occur attached to a root or word. In an agglutinative language, affixes are very important. They take part in the formation of various words and in deriving several word class, namely, noun, verb, adjective and adverb. Beside these, they are used in forming various sentence types- declarative, negative, interrogative and imperative.

There are two types of affixes in Chothe i.e. prefix and suffix. They are discussed in the following.

Prefixes:-

Chothe has the pronominal prefix only which are affixed to the nominal as the indicator of the prossessor of the noun concerned. Nominal pronominalization is the characteristic feature of the Chothe. In the nominal pronominalization, the pronominal prefixes may be treated as the abbreviated forms of the personal pronouns with the meaning of possessive pronouns, which are affixed in the nominal form itself to specify the possessor of the noun concerned. There are three types of pronominal prefixes. They are given in the following:-

(a) **kə** - 'first person'

(b) **nə** - 'second person'

(c) **ə-/mə-** 'third person'

kə-

The possessor of the first person singular is indicated by the prefix **kə-** 'my' an abbreviated form of **kəy** 'I' personal pronoun of the first person singular.

Examples:-

1. (a) kə-may (b) kə-lu (c) kə-hoŋ
   pp-face pp-head pp-neck
   'my face' 'my head' 'my neck'

nə-

The possessor of the second person is indicated by the prefix **nə-** 'you' an abbreviated form of **nəŋ** 'you'.

Examples:-

2. (a) nə -ha (b) nə -hu (c) nə-ke
   pp-teeth pp-village pp-leg
   'your teeth' 'your village' 'your leg'

ə-/mə-

The possessor of the third person singular is indicated by the prefix **ə-** or **mə-** 'his/her/its' an abbreviated form of **əmo** 'he/her/it'. The prefix **mə-** is familiar to the native speaker of Chothe.

Examples:-

3. (a) mə-hoŋ (b) mə-lu (c) mə-ha
   pp-leg pp-head pp-teeth
   'his/her/its leg' 'his/her/its head' 'his/her/its teeth'

There are some different forms to indicate the possessor. They are as follows:-

(i) Personal pronoun + ta + e/ye

(ii) Pronominal prefix + ta + e/ye

Examples:-

4. (a) aytok-ha kəy-ta-ye
   duck-ddet. I-gen.-SP
   'That duck is mine.'

(b) aytok-ha kə-ta-ye
duck-ddet pp-gen.-SP
'That duck is mine.'

In the above examples, as in (4a, b) the two forms i.e. **kəy-ta-ye** "I, genitive marker and SP" (i.e. mine) and **kə-ta-ye** "pronominal prefix, genitive marker and SP" (i.e. mine) are treated as the same meaning in this environment. These two forms may be treated as the possessive pronouns.

Suffixes

The affixes which can occur after the root are known as suffixes. There are many suffixes which are more than the number of prefixes. Suffixes can be divided into two categories i.e. (a) nominal suffixes and (b) Verbal suffixes. They are discussed in the following.

Nominal suffixes

Nominal suffixes are very large in number. They are plural markers, diminutive marker, case marker, gender marker etc.

Number Suffixes

In Chothe, the suffixes – **ni** , -ŋəy, **-yam** etc. are used as a number suffix for indicating plural marker. The word **ətəmmə, jura, əboy/əkuy, honnə, milim, əhu, bommə, ətəy** etc. are used as a collective number (see for detail in number).

Diminutive suffixes

In common gender, the diminutive suffix **-te** is used to indicate small animals, for instance, **site** 'calf' **uyte** 'puppy' **əkete** 'kid' **okte** 'piglet',etc.

There are two different sets of suffixes to indicate male and female; the suffix **-pa** for male and **-pinu** for female in the lexical items of birds and animals respectively. In the case of insects, male and female are indicated by words or by adding suffixing markers, namely **əpa** for male and **-pinu** for female for indicating the gender system of insects as a lexical item. In addressing the respected man and woman, **-pu** and **-pi/-nu** are used as suffixes of respected man and woman respectively (see for detail in gender).

Case suffixes

There are seven case suffixes. They are nominative case –**nə**, accusative case –**tə**, genitive case **-ta**, instrumental case –**nə**, locative case **-ke/-keya**, ablative case **-kena** and associative case **-rit** (see for detail in case).

The suffix –**cək** is added to a noun to indicate 'only'. Some examples are givenbelow:-

əncək	'only curry'
tuycək	'only water'
bucək	'only rice'
səŋkomcək	'only milk'

Verbal suffixes

Chothe has many kinds of verbal suffixes. It can be mentioned that different grammatical properties are indicated by the respective suffixes. Tense or aspects are indicated by their respective suffixes (see Tense or Aspect). The nominalizer –**pə** and the honorific marker **-pi** can be suffixed to the verbal roots. Subordinating conjunction are also suffixed to the verbal roots (see surbordinating conjunctions). In this language, declarative, negative, interrogative and imperative sentences are all constructed by the suffixation of respective markers to the verbal roots (see Sentence process). Reciprocal and togetherness suffixes can be suffixed to the verbal roots.

THREE

Noun Categories

Gender

"Genders are classes of nouns reflected in the behaviour of associated words. To qualify as a gender system, the classification must be exhaustive and much not involve extensive intersection; that is, every noun must belong to one of the classes, and very few can belong to more than one", (Hockett,1958).

Gender and sex are often associated together. "The traditional names for the three genders found in the classical Indo-European language- "masculine", "faminine" and "neuter" - clearly reflect the association which traditional grammar established between sex and gender. But the term "gender" itself derives from an extremely general word meaning "class" or "kind" (Latin **genus**):- the three gender of Greek and Latin were the three main noun-classes recognized in the grammar. From the grammatical point of view, the nouns of Greek and Latin were classified into three genders in order to account for two distinct phenomena:- (a) Pronominal reference and (b) adjective concord (or "agreement"). For the same reasons, the nouns of French, Italian and Spanish are classified into two genders, the nouns of Russian and German into three genders, the nouns of Swahili into at least six gender, and so on," (Lyons, 1968).

Gender is only a lexical feature in Chothe. It has no role in showing grammatical relationship between the nouns and other categories in the sentences. In the other words, Chothe has no grammatical gender, it has only natural gender.

This is substantiated by the following examples:-

1. (a) əpa-te akʰa tan-nəm-me
man-small one run-CON.asp.-SP
'A boy is running.'

(b) numəy-te əkʰa tan-nəm-me
female-small one run-CON.asp-SP
'A girl is running.'

2. (a) ə-tʰa-pə əpa-te əkʰa lək-kəm-me
FP-good-NZ man-small one play-CON.asp-SP
'A good boy is playing.'

(b) ə-tʰa-pə numəy-te əkʰa lək-kəm-me
FP-good-NZ female-small one play-CON.asp-SP
'A good girl is playing.'

The adjective **ə-tʰa-pə** 'good' and the verb **lək-kəm-me** 'is playing' remain unchanged when they occur with the different opposite sexes **əpate** 'boy' and **numəyte** 'girl'. They have no role in showing grammatical relationship between the noun **əpate** and **numəyte** in the above sentences.

Lexical Opposites

I. Human Beings

There are some nouns which can denote either male or female but do not possess any generic name. In this case of these nouns, words indicate the opposite sex either male or female.

Examples:-

		Male	Female
3.	(a)	əpa 'man'	numəy 'woman'
	(b)	kə-pa pp-father 'my father'	kə-nu pp-mother 'my mother'

(c)	ə-sənaw-pa pp-child-male 'his son'	ə-sənaw-nu pp-child-female 'his daughter'

In the case of nouns having generic names, male and female are indicated by the suffix **-pa/pu** 'male' and **-nu/pi** 'female' to the generic names.

Examples:-

	Generic name	Male	Female
4.	(a) suk 'slave'	suk-pa 'male slave'	suk-nu 'female slave'
	(b) $ət^{h}im$ 'local physician'	$ət^{h}im$-pa/pu 'male local physician,	$ət^{h}im$-nu/pi 'female local physician'
	(c) lò 'festival organiser for custom'	lò-pa 'male festival organiser'	lò-nu/pi 'female festival organisor'

II. Animals and birds

In Chothe, male and female are indicated by adding words or by suffing markers, namely, **-pa** for 'male', **-pinu** for 'female' in the lexical items of birds and animals. They are given below:-

Animal

Examples:-

	Generic name	Male	Female
5.	(a) ləm-uy 'fox'	ləm-uy-pa 'male fox'	ləm-uy-pinu 'female fox'
	(b) əkəy 'tiger'	əkəy-pa 'male tiger'	əkəy-pinu 'female tiger'
	(c) səkoy 'horse'	səkoy-pa 'male horse'	səkoy-pinu 'female horse'

Birds

Examples:-

	Generic name	Male	Female
6.	(a) əwa 'bird'	əwa-pa 'male bird'	əwa-pinu 'female bird'
	(b) pʰəyboy 'nightingale'	pʰəyboy-pa 'nightingale(M)'	pʰəyboy-pinu 'nightingale(F)'
	(c) aytok 'duck'	aytok-pa 'male duck'	aytok-pinu 'female duck'

III. Insects

In the case of insects, male and female are indicated by adding words or by suffixing markers, namely **əpa** for 'male' and **-pinu** for 'female' for indicating the gender system of insects as a lexical item.

Examples:-

	Generic name	Male	Female
7.	(a) tʰəw 'fly'	tʰəw-əpa 'male fly'	tʰəw-pinu 'female fly'
	(b) lik 'louse'	lik-əpa 'male louse'	lik-pinu 'female louse'
	(c) haw 'locust'	haw-əpa 'male locust'	haw-pinu 'female locust'

IV. Plants

In Chothe, **əpa** and **numəy** are used to the generic item of plants for indicating the gender system of plants as a lexical item. They are given below:-

Examples:-

	Generic name	Male	Female
8.	(a) t^{h}əytup 'apple'	t^{h}əytup-əpa 'male apple'	t^{h}əytup-numəy 'female apple'
	(b) t^{h}əyk^{h}a 'plum'	t^{h}əyk^{h}a-əpa 'male plum'	t^{h}əyk^{h}a-numəy 'female plum'
	(c) t^{h}əycəŋ 'a fruit'	t^{h}əycəŋ-əpa 'a fruit (M)'	t^{h}əycəŋ-numəy 'a fruit (F)'

Number

Number is a category of the noun. Its most common manifestation is the distinction between plural and singular which rests upon recognition of persons, animals and objects which can be counted and referred to by means of nouns.

In Chothe, number is not a grammatical category. It will be clear from the examples given below:-

9. (a) əpa-te-hi t^{h}a-ye
man-small-pdet. good-SP
'This boy is good.'

(b) əpa-te-ŋəy-hi t^{h}a-ye
man-small-pl-pdet good-SP
'These boys are good.'

10. (a) əbay-hi t^{h}a-ye
book-pdet good-SP
'This book is good.'

(b) əbay-ŋəy-hi t^{h}a-ye
book-pl-pdet good-SP
'These books are good.'

Chothe has the plural formation of nouns, plurals of personal pronouns and plural formation of demonstrative pronouns. They are dicussed in the following.

A. Plural formation of nouns

I. Suffixation of the plural marker -ŋəy

The plural marker -ŋəy can be added to the noun or a word conveying the idea of plurality to make a plural.

Examples:-

		Singular	Plural
11.	(a)	mi 'man'	mi-ŋəy 'men'
	(b)	si 'cow'	si-ŋəy 'cows'
	(c)	uy 'dog'	uy-ŋəy 'dogs'

II. Suffixation of the plural marker **-yam**

To make the plural formation, the plural marker **-yam** can be suffixed to the noun or a word conveying the idea of plurality.

Examples:-

		Singular	Plural
12.	(a)	mi 'man'	mi-yam 'many men'
	(b)	si 'cow'	si-yam 'many cows'
	(c)	uy 'dog'	uy-yam 'many dogs'

III. Addition of words

In Chothe, the words indicating plurality are-**ətəmmə** 'all', **jura** 'pair', **əboy/əkuy** 'bunch', **honnə** 'heap/pile', **milim** 'crowd', **əhù** 'bundle', **bommə** 'group', **ətəy** 'some', etc.

Examples:-

		Singular	Plural
13.	(a)	si 'cow'	si-ətəmmə 'all cows'
	(b)	əbay 'book'	əbay-ətəy 'some book'
	(c)	saŋ 'paddy'	saŋ-honnə 'heap of paddy'
	(d)	t^hayk^ha (tʰəykʰa) 'plum'	tʰəykʰa-əboy 'bunch of plum'
	(e)	pun 'cloth'	pun-əhù 'bundle of cloth'
	(f)	mi 'man'	mi-bommə 'group of men'

B. Plural of personal pronouns

The suffixed **-ni/-ŋəy** is the plural marker of the personal pronouns in Chothe.

Examples:-

14.	Singular	Plural
	kəy 'I'	kə-ni/ə-ni 'we'
	nəŋ 'you'	nə-ni/nə-ŋəy 'you(pl)'
	əmo 'he/she/it'	mə-ni/mə-ŋəy 'they'

C. Plural formation of demonstrative pronouns

To demonstrate is 'to point out'. These pronouns point out persons or things.

Examples:-

15. **Singular** **Plural**

hi-na-hi 'it'	hi-na-ŋəy-hi 'these'
ha-na-ha 'that'	ha-na-ŋəy-ha 'those'

Case

"Cases are inflected forms for nouns which fit them for participation in key constructions relative to verbs", (Hockett, 1985). Case is the most important inflectional category of the noun. In other words of Crytal (1985) Case is "a grammatical category" used in the analysis of word classes to identify the syntatic relationship between words in a sentence throgh such contrasts as nominative, accusative, etc.

Generally, case is defined in traditional grammers as "the relation in which a noun stands to some other word, or change of form (if any) by which this relation is indicated grammatical relation as well as the change of form".

In Chothe, there are seven cases. The nominative case **–nə** is homophonous with the instrumental case **–nə**. They are given below:-

Nominative	-nə
Accusative	-tə
Genitive	-ta
Instrumental	-nə
Locative	-ke/keyə
Ablative	-kena
Associative	-rit

I. Nominative

The most widely accepted function of nominative is to mark the subject of the sentence. It is expressed by the suffix **-nə**, the most important function of this suffix is to differentiate the agent from the object in sentences in which both are used side by side.

Examples:-

16. (a)	dimho-nə	tʰahoy	huk-ke
	Dimo-nom.	Thahoi	beat-SP
	'Dimho beats Thaoi.'		
(b)	tʰahoy	dimho-nə	huk-ke
	Thahoi	Dimho-nom.	beat-SP
	'Dimho beats Thahoi.'		
17. (a)	əmo-nə	bu-ha	bək-ke
	he/she/it-nom.	rice-ddet.	eat-SP
	'He/She/It eats rice.'		
(b)	bu-ha	əmo-nə	bək-ke
	rice-ddet.	he/she/it-nom.	eat-SP
	'He/She/It eats rice.'		

But in the other contexts, the used of this suffix **–nə** is optional. The suffix **–nə** has an additional meaning i.e. the action of the subject is more emphasis. In the case of transitive verbs, the nominative suffix **–nə** is not primarily used to mark the agent when the subject precedes the object.

Examples:-

Transitive verb

18. (a)	kəy	əmo	dəŋ-ŋe
	I	he	know-SP
	'I know him.'		
(b)	coŋte	tuy	in-ne
	Chongte	water	drink-SP
	'Chongte drinks water.'		

In the case of intransitive verbs and stative verbs also the nominative suffix **–nə** is not used.

Examples:-

Intransitive verb

19.	(a)	əmo	əsaŋ	t^{h}iŋ-ŋe
		he/she/it	Imphal	go-SP
		'He/She/It goes to Imphal.'		
	(b)	əmo	kəyt^{h}i	t^{h}iŋ-ŋe
		he/she/it	market	go-SP
		'He/She/It goes to market.'		

Stative verb

20..	(a)	əmo	dəŋ-ŋe
		he/she/it	know-SP
		'He/She/It knows.'	
	(b)	nəŋ	siŋ-ŋe
		you	wise-SP
		'You are wise.'	

The nominative suffix **–nə** is used in the exclusive meaning, comparison and contrastive focus.

Examples:-

Exlcusive

21..	(a)	uŋa-nə	əbay	əwray-yəm-me
		child-nom.	book	read-CON.asp.-SP

'The child is reading the book (while others were doing something).'

(b)	kəy-nə	əmo	huk-ke
	I-nom.	he	beat-SP
	'Ibeat him (while others were playing).'		

Comparison

22.	t^{h}ahoy-nə	ənt^{h}a-ye
	Thahoi-nom.	beautiful-SP
	'Thahoi is beautiful (than someone).'	

Contrastive focus

23.	coŋte-nə	in-ne	tʰahoy-nə	bək-ke
	Chongte-nom	drink-SP	Thahoi-nom.	eat-SP

'Chongte drinks (something) while Thahoi eats something.'

In the above example (23), the nominative suffix **–nə** is used as a distributive or specified meaning.

II. Accusative

The accusative suffix is primarily used for denoting the direct object of a transitive verb. The accusative suffix of Chothe is **"tə"**. It may or may not be used, but if used, it carries some emphatic sence.

Examples:-

24.	(a)	əmo-nə	kəy-tə	kok-ke
		he-nom.	I-acc.	call-SP
		'He calls me (but not others).'		
	(b)	əmo-nə	kəy	kok-ke
		he-nom.	I	call-SP
		'He calls me.'		
25.	(a)	kəy –nə	əmo-tə	huk-ke
		I-nom.	he-acc.	beat-SP
		'I beat him (but not others).'		
	(b)	kəy-nom.	əmo	huk-ke
		I-nom.	he	beat-SP
		'I beat him.'		

The particle **–cək** 'only' is used to the exclusive meaning, to indicate some amount of extra emphasis of the object. The determiner **-hi** or **-ha** indicates to mark definiteness with reference to the object.

Examples:-

A. Exclusive **–cək**

26.	kəy-nə	əmo-cək	liŋləy-ye
	I-nom.	he-excl.	love-SP

'I love him only (while I don't love others).'

B. Emphasis **-hi/-ha**

27. (a) kəy-nə əmo-hi liŋləy-ye
I-nom. he-pdet love-SP
'I love him (who is here).'

(b) kəy-nə əmo-ha liŋləy-ye
I-nom. he-ddet love-SP
'I love him (who is there).'

III. Genitive

The genitive case is the possessive relationship. In Chothe, genitive case can be seen in two ways - (a) one in which the genitive suffix is affixed to nouns or pronouns as in the examples (28a-b) and (b) the genitive suffix is affixed to the pronominal markers (prefix) or pronouns as in the examples (29a-b).

Examples:-

28. (a) hi-na-hi t^{h}ahoy-ta pun-ne
pdet-away-pdet Thahoi-gen. cloth-SP
"This is Thahoi's cloth."

(b) əmo dimho-ta ə-sənaw-we
he Dimho-gen. att.-child-SP
"He is Dimho's son."

29. (a) əbay-hi kə-ta-ye
book-pdet pp.-gen.-SP
"This book belongs to me."

(b) liŋlut-hi nəŋ-ta-ye
shirt-pdet you-gen.-SP
"This shirt is yours."

The genitive suffix **-ta** is suffixed to the pronominal markers or pronouns (see possessive pronouns).

There is another structure, the genitive marker **-ta** is not used to the pronouns but it carries the genitive relationship.

Examples:-

30.	(a) kə-pa	(b) nə-pa	(c) mə-pa
	pp-father	pp-father	pp-father
	'My father'	'Your father'	'His father'
	(d) kəni-pa	(e) nəni-pa	(f) məni-pa
	our-father	your-father	their-father
	'Our father'	'Your(pl) father'	'Their father'

IV. Instrumental

The instrumental suffix **–nə** is to mark the instrument used by the agent while an activity is being carried out (by noun or pronoun).

Examples:-

31.	(a) əmo-nə	kaydi-tə	t^hiŋtən-nə	huk-ke
	he-nom.	kaidi-acc.	stick-int.	beat-SP
	'He beats kaidi with a stick.'			
	(b) kəy-nə	əruy-tə	əruŋ-nə	t^hət-te
	I-nom.	snake-acc.	stone-int.	kill-SP
	'I kill the snake with a stone.'			

In Chothe, the suffix⁻ **-nə** can be used to denote the cause of state like **ci** 'wet' **na** 'ill' etc.

Examples:-

32.	(a) əmo	ətunt^{h}əwa-nə	na-ye
	he	fever-with	ill-SP
	'He is ill with fever.'		
	(b) əmo	tuy-nə	ci-ye
	he	water-with	wet-SP
	'He is wet with water.'		

It is also used to denote the material used for making certain objects or construction purposes.

Example:-

33.	kəy-nə	t^{h}iŋ-nə	ìn	say-ye
	I-nom.	wood-with	house	make-SP

'I built a house with wood.'

And, as an extension, it is used to denote the medium for such activities as cooking, painting, etc.

Examples:-

34.	(a)	əmo-nə	si-ek-nə	bu	kəm-me
		he-nom	cow-dung-with	rice	cook-SP

'He cooks rice with cow-dung.'

	(b)	əmo-nə	ìnbəŋ-ha	ədikpə-nə	təy-ye
		he-nom.	wall-ddet	green-with	paint-SP

'He paints that wall with green colour.'

V. Locative

The locative suffix is to indicate the locative of an object or event. The locative suffix **-ke** is to indicate only a simple location but the suffix **–keyə** is used in more emphatic sense (definilization). The term location may be used in two different senses. They are:- (a) Spatial orientation of an action or a state, etc. and (b) Spatial end point of a direction or motion. They are discussed in the following.

The locative suffix **-ke/-keyə** occurs in the spatial orientation of an action or a state, etc.

Examples:-

35.	(a)	kolom-ha	tebəl-ke	əm-me
		pen-ddet.	table-loc.	live-SP

'That pen is on the table.'

	(b)	kolom-ha	tebəl-keyə	əm-me
		pen-ddet.	table-loc.	live-SP

'That pen is on the table (emphatic).'

The locative suffix **-ke/-keyə** occurs in the spatial end point of a direction or motion.

Examples:-

36. (a) əmo əsaŋ-ke tʰiŋ-ŋe
he Imphal-loc go-SP
'He goes to Imphal.'

(b) əmo əsaŋ-keyə tʰiŋ-ŋe
he Imphal-loc go-SP
'He goes to Imphal (emphatic).'

VI. Ablative

This refers to the form taken by a word, usually a noun or pronoun typically used in the expression of range of locative meaning. "A case form which typically indicates the source of a movement: Turkish **evden** 'from the house' (**ev** 'house')"; (Trask,1993). It is used in the spatial starting point of a direction or motion.

Examples:-

37. (a) əmo moyraŋ-kena əsaŋ-ke wa-ye
he Moirang-abl. Imphal-loc. come-SP
'He comes from Moirang to Imphal.'

(b) əmo kəytʰi-kena wa-ye
he market-abl come-SP
'He comes from market.'

VII. Associative

The primary function of the associative suffix **-rit** is to denote an individual or object in whose association the agent is carrying out an activity.

Examples:-

38. (a) kəy-nə bu-ha ŋa-rit bək-ke
I-nom rice-ddet fish-asso. eat-SP
'I eat that rice with fish.'

(b)	kəy-nə	haw-ha	əmo-rit	lon-wa-ye
	I-nom.	bag-ddet	he-asso.	carry- come-SP

'I carry that bag with him.'

(c)	kəy	əmo-rit	kəyt^hi	t^hiŋ-ŋe
	I	he-asso.	market	go-SP

'I go to the market with him.'

Case Role

In a given sentence, noun or pronoun or noun phrases have the exact roles that each of them plays in the action or event denoted by the verb. "The kind of case roles that can occur in a given sentence depends primarily upon the kind of verb or predicate that has been used in it (Bhat and Ningomba, 1995). On the basis of the case roles, the minimum exact number of the distinct individuals or object to be reffered to in the given sentence can be fixed. For instance, if a verb like **ənt^ha-ye** "beautiful + SP" and **waŋ-ŋe** "tall + SP" are used, there would be a need to denote at least only a single case role, namely a person or an object in order to express a complete idea connected with the verb of the sentence.

Examples:-

39.	(a)	əmo	ənt^ha-ye
		he	beautiful-SP

'He is beautiful.'

	(b)	mi-ha	waŋ-ŋe
		man-ddet	tall-SP

'That man is tall.'

The verbs like **ən-ne** "look + SP" , **e-ye** " do + SP" etc. are used to indicate at least two different case roles namely an actor (the person who looks or does) and an object (the thing that the actor looks or does).

Examples:-

40.	(a)	əmo-nə	dimho	ən-ne
		he-nom.	Dimho	look-SP

'He looks Dimho.'

(b) əmo-nə tulu-hi e-ye
he-nom work-pdet do-SP
'He does this work.'

Then, the verbs like **pe-ye** "give + SP" , **la-ye** "take + SP" , **juy-ye** "sell + SP" etc. are used to indicate at least three different case roles, namely, an actor, an object and also a beneficiary (the person to whom something is given or sold).

Examples:-

41. (a) əmo-nə dimho-ke liŋlut əkʰa pe-ye
he-nom. Dimho-loc. shirt one give-SP
'He gives a shirt to Dimho.'

(b) nəŋ-nə dimho-ke pun əkʰa juy-ye
you-nom. Dimho-loc. cloth one sell-SP
'You sell a cloth to Dimho.'

From the above examples, as in (41a-b), it is noticed that the number and kind of case roles that can occur depend upon the type of the verb in the given sentence.

NUMERALS

In Chothe, "numeral is a word or phrase denoting a number". Broadly, numeral can be classified into two categories; viz (a) Cardinal numbers and (b) Ordinal numbers. Cardinal numbers have more complex and more formal structures whereas the ordinal numbers are very simple in the formation of their structures. They are dicussed in the following.

CARDINAL NUMBERS

Cardinal numbers are used in counting, showing how many objects are specified as one, two, three, etc. It has two types:- (i) Basic numerals and (ii) Compound numerals.

BASIC NUMERALS

There are twelve basic numerals. They are 1 to 10, 100 and 1000.

Examples:-

42.	əkʰa	'one'	səri	'seven'
	əni	'two'	əret	'eight'
	intʰum	'three'	əku	'nine'
	inli	'four'	əsom	'ten'
	rəŋa	'five'	liha	'hundred'
	əruk	'six'	lisiŋ	'thousand'

COMPOUND NUMERALS

There are three types of compound numerals. They are:- (a) additive compound (b) multiplicative compound and (c) multiplicative-cum- additive compound.

Additive Compound Numerals

The numerals from eleven to nineteen are additive compound numerals. It has no special marker. They are formed by adding the basic numerals to the **əsom** "ten" i.e. 10+1, 10+2, 10+3, ...etc.

Examples:-

43.	əsoməkʰa	'eleven'	əsoməruk	'sixteen'
	əsoməni	'twelve'	əsomsəri	seventeen'
	əsomintʰum	'thirteen'	əsoməret	'eighteen'
	əsominli	'fourteen'	əsoməku	'nineteen'
	əsomrəŋa	'fifteen'		

Multiplicative Compound Numerals

There are two types of multiplicative compound numerals. They are (i) Lower multiplicative and (ii) Higher multiplicative compound numerals.

Lower Multiplicative Compound Numerals

The lower multiplicative compounds are twenty, thirty forty, fifty, sixty, seventy, eighty and ninety. It is formed as 10 X basic numerals. In this numeral, the first syllable ə- of **ə-som** "ten", **ə-ni** "two", **ə-ruk** "six", **ə-ret** "eight" and **ə-ku** "nine" of basic numerals have been dropped. Then the first syllable **in**- of **in-tʰum** "three" and **in-li** "four" of the basic numerals are also dropped. Again, the syllable **rə**- of **rə-ŋa** "five" of the basic numeral has been dropped. But in the case of the basic numeral **sə-ri** "seven", the first syllable **sə**- is not dropped in Chothe.

Examples:-

44.	somni	'twenty'	somruk	'sixty'
	somtʰum	'thirty'	somsəri	'seventy'
	somli	'forty'	somret	'eighty'
	somŋa	'fifty'	somku	'ninety'

Higher Multiplicative Compound Numerals

There are two types of higher multiplicative compound numerals. They are:- century and thousand. The **liha** "hundred" and **lisiŋ** "thousand" are the root of the hundred and thousand respectively. In the case of century, the basic numerals are suffixed to the **liha** "hundred" i.e. root of century. Then the first syllable ə- of **ə-kʰa** "one", **ə-ni** "two", **ə-ruk** "six", **ə-ret** "eight" and **ə-ku** "nine"; the first syllable **in**- of **in-tʰum** "three", **in-li** "four" and the first syllable **rə**- of **rə-ŋa** "five" of basic numerals heave been dropped.

Examples:-

45.	lihakʰa	'one hundred'
	lihani	'two hundred'
	lihatʰum	'three hundred'
	lihali	'four hundred'
	lihaŋa	'five hundred'
	liharuk	'six hundred'
	lihasəri	'seven hundred'
	liharet	'eight hundred'
	lihaku	'nine hundred', etc.

But in the case of thousand, there is no question of dropping the first syllable of the basic numerals as in century.

Examples:-

46.	lisiŋəkʰə	'one thousand'
	lisiŋəni	'two thousand'
	lisiŋintʰum	'three thousand'
	lisiŋinli	'four thousand'
	lisiŋrəŋa	'five thousand'
	lisiŋəruk	'six thousand'
	lisiŋsəri	'seven thousand'
	lisiŋəret	'eight thousand'
	lisiŋəku	'nine thousand', etc.

Multiplicative-cum-Additive Compound Numerals

The numerals from 21 to 29, 31 to 39, 41 to 49, 51 to 59, 61 to 69, 71 to 79, 81 to 89, 91 to 99, 101 to 110, 201 to 210, 301 to 310, 401 to 410, 501 to 510, 601 to 610, 702 to 710, etc. are all multiplicative-cum-additive compound numerals.

There are three forms of multiplicative-cum-additive numerals. They are as follows:-

I. Decade X basic numerals + basic numerals

II. Century X basic numerals + **rit** + basic numerals

III. Lising X basic numerals + **rit** + basic numerals

I. Decade X Basic Numerals + Basic Numerals

Examples:-

47.	somni əkʰa	'twenty one'
	somni əni	'twenty two'
	somni intʰum	'twenty three'

somni inli 'twenty four'
somni rəŋa 'twenty five'
somni əruk 'twenty six'
somni səri 'twenty seven'
somni əret 'twenty eight'
somni əku 'twenty nine'

II. Century X Basic Numerals + rit + Basic Numerals

In this case, **rit** is used as a connective for the formation of this type of numerals i.e. century X basic numerals + **rit** + basic numerals.

Examples:-

48. lihak^{h}arit ək^{h}a 'one hundred and one'
lihak^{h}arit əni 'one hundred and two'
lihak^{h}arit int^{h}um 'one hundred and three'
lihak^{h}arit inli 'one hundred and four'
lihak^{h}arit rəŋa 'one hundred and five'
lihak^{h}arit əruk 'one hundred and six'
lihak^{h}arit səri 'one hundred and seven'
lihak^{h}arit əret 'one hundred and eight'
lihak^{h}arit əku 'one hundred and nine'
lihak^{h}arit əsom 'one hundred and ten'

III. Lising(thousand) X Basic Numeral + rit + Basic Numerals

In this type, **rit** is used as a connective for the formation of this type of numerals i.e. **lising** (thousand) X basic numeral + **rit** + basic numerals.

Examples:-

49. lisiŋ ək^{h}arit ək^{h}a 'one thousand and one'
lisiŋ ənirit əni 'two thousand and two'
lisiŋ int^{h}umrit int^{h}um 'three thousand and three'
lisiŋ inlirit inli 'four thousand and four'

Repetition/Distribution Numerals

There is a complete reduplication of the cardinal numerals. It is used as distributive numerals.

Examples:-

50.	əkʰa əkʰa	'one each'
	əni əni	'two each'
	intʰum intʰum	'there each'
	inli inli	'four each'
	əret əret	'eight each', etc.

Multiplicative Numerals

Multiplicatives are derived from the cardinal numerals. It is used when a question arises "how many times and how many folds". The prefix **woy-** and suffix **-ret/-let** are used in the formation of the multiplicative numerals.

Examples:-

51.	woykʰaret	'once/single time'
	woyniret	'twice/double times'
	woytʰumlet	'three times'
	woyliret	'four times',etc.

Aggregative Numerals

In Chothe, the suffix **-lin** is used as a marker of aggregative numerals. It expresses the meaning "two together or both", "three together or all the three", etc.

Examples:-

52.	ənilin	'two together or both'
	intʰumlin	'all the three'
	əret lin	'all the eight'
	əsomlin	'all the ten', etc.

Approximate Numerals

The suffix **–cək** is used as a marker of the approximative numerals. It gives an approximate in counting.

Examples:-

53. əkʰacək 'about one'
    ənicək 'about two'
    inlicək 'about four'
    əretcək 'about eight', etc.

The word **nore** "or" is also used as an approximate numeral.

Examples:-

54. əni nore intʰum 'two or three'
    inli nore rəŋa 'four or five'
    əret nore əsom 'eight or ten', etc.

Fractional Numerals

The suffix **-suŋŋa** is the marker of the fractional numerals. It is used in the polymorphemic, but it is not used in the morphemic fraction **əhuy** "half". It denotes the fraction of the wholes, as quarter, three quarter, etc.

Examples:-

55. əhuy 'half'
    intʰum suŋŋa əkʰa 'one-third'
    inli suŋŋa əkʰa 'one-fourth'
    inli suŋŋa intʰum 'three-fourth'

Ordinal Numerals

Ordinal numbers are derived from the cardinal numbers by adding the suffix **–supə** to the cardinal number except the **misapə** "first".

Examples:-

56.	ənisupə	'second'
	int^{h}umsupə	'third'
	inlisupə	'fourth'
	rəŋasupə	'fifth', etc.

FOUR

VERBAL CATEGORIES

Verb

"The Formal definition of a verb refers to an element which can display Morphological contrasts of tense, aspect, voice, mood, person and number. Functionally, it is an element which, single or combination with other verbs (i.e. "verb phrase"), is used as the minimal predicate of a sentence, co-occurring with a subject e.g. he/came. If the predicate contains other elements (e.g. object, complement, adverbial), then it is the verb which more than any other is the unit which influences the choice and extent of these elements; e.g. the verb **put** takes both an object and a locative adverbial, as in **he put the book on the table.** In many grammatical theories, the verb is considered the most important element in sentence structure"; (Crystal, 1985).

In Chothe, verb is the most important component in the formation of a sentence. It can be classified into three main types on the basis of semantics, namely, (a) action verb (b) process verb and (c) stative verb. They are discussed below:-

Action Verbs

in	'drink'
bək	'eat'
t^hiŋ	'go'
hut	'write'
yuŋ	'fly'
t^hət	'kill', etc.

Their occurrence in the sentences are given below:-

1. (a) kəy bu bək-ke
I cook rice eat-SP
'I eat cook rice.'

(b) əmo iskul t^hiŋ-ŋe
he school go-SP
'He goes to school.'

Process Verb

kəm	'cook'
əy	'ache'
min	'ripe'
jap	'blow'
taw	'float'

Their occurrence in the sentences are given in the following examples.

2. (a) əmo ən kəm-me
he curry cook-SP
'He cooks curry.'

(b) t^həyhay-ha min-ne
mango-ddet ripe-SP
That mango is ripe.'

(c) kəy-ta ha əy-ye
I-gen. teeth ache-SP
'My teeth is ache.'

Stative Verbs.

day	'cold'
rok	'big'
sin	'small'
rit	'heavy'
t^ha	'good'

Their occurrence in the sentences are given below:-

3. (a) t^hiŋ-ha rok-ke
tree-ddet big-SP
'That tree is big.'

(b) liŋlut-hi sin-ne
shirt-pdet small-SP
'This shirt is small.'

(c) tomba t^ha-ye
Tomba good-SP
'Tomba is good.'

Formation of Verb

In Chothe, verbs are formed by the suffixation of aspect markers and occur finally in a sentence with sentence partical(SP).

Examples:-

4. (a) kəy t^hiŋ-ŋəŋ-ŋe
I go-UNR.asp-SP
'I will go.'

(b) əmo bu bək-səw-we
he cook rice eat-PER.asp-SP
'He has taken his meal.'

In the above example (4a), **t^hiŋ-ŋəŋ-ŋe** "will go" is an instransitive verb and in the examples (4b), **bək-səw-we** "has taken" is the transitive verb. Verbs are stems that convey the object reference in the case of transitive verbs. In intransitive verbs, the object reference does not arise.

Auxiliary Verb

The suffix -ŋəy is the auxiliary verb in Chothe. It is suffixed to the verbal roots and it makes a set of verbs.

Examples:-

5. (a) kəy bək-ŋay-ye

I eat-may-SP
'I may eat.'

(b) əmo wa-ŋay-ye
he come-may-SP
'He may come.'

Verb "BE"

Recent developments in the theory of grammar are towards a maximally general from the rules (cf. Katz and Fodor, 1963; Chomsky, 1965; Bach, 1967). In this connection the often despised problem of linguistic universals has acquired new position (cf. Greenberg, 1963; Weinreich, 1963 and 1966).

Lyons (1968) considers verb "be" not as a constituent of deep structure, but semantically empty "dummy verb". Meillet (1938) focussing on the nonsemantic form of verb "be" says that verb "be" is a grammatical device used for introducing the markers of aspect, tense, mood and person in a sentence.

Bach (1967) proposes an analysis in which he eliminates verb "be" (and "have") as a main verb from the base and derives it transformationally. He brings out some minor additions to the Chomskian base rules (1965) in which Chomsky had retained the copula in the base. The new base rules, he proposed, are closer to the universal base rule as compared to the rules proposed in the earlier analysis.

Thus, most of the linguist consider the copulative function of verb "be" a secondary "development" and, therefore, it should be eliminated from the base and should be derived transformationally. All the views presented above, take case of only a part of the problem. We cannot account for both the copulation "be" and the "be" present in existential constructions (EC) in the same way. We cannot derive verb "be" in EC through transformations for the simple reason that the fuction of verb "be" in EC is different from its copulative function. Gilson's argument as reported in Kahn (1973), is an evidence for the fact that the status of verb "be" in EC is that of a main verb, with semantic content.

Keeping in view the status of the verb "be" in various constructions ranging from EC to copula constructions, it may be claimed that verb "be" has basic functions:-

(I) In EC, it is present in the base because in (EC) verb "be" functions as a main verb and with full semantic content.

(II) In a non-existential constructions (non-EC), it is inserted at a later stage through transformations. Non-EC include copulative, auxiliary, locative, possessive constructions (PS). The function of verb "be" as a copula is that of a linker.

In EC verb "be" asserts or negates the existence of an object X, and thus, it has a semantic value. In locative construction (LC), however, it serves as a linker only. Similarly, in PS verb "be" acts merely as a linker between the two NPs- the possessor and possessed.

According to Bhaskarao (1972), Telugu verb "be" has two types of predications- Existential and Copulative. He establishes three types of existential constructions:-(a) Absolute existential construction (b) Temporal existential construction, and (c) Locative existential construction.

The most characteristic feature of verb "be" is "stativity". So on this basis, we may say that verb "be" (i) defines a singular state, not a change from state X to Y, and (ii) may show the continuance or progress of a singular state, and not the derived state which is a result of a change (Boadi,1969).

Verb "be" has multiple functions to perform in various types of constructions in the language of the world. These functions which range from copulative to existentia' are strikingly diverse in nature. They do not exibit any apparent relation among themselves.

Russell(1903) pointed out four functions of verb "be", namely, existence,predication, identity and class inclusion. Later, locative and possessive constructions are also added to these functions. But these are not the only functions that verb "be" performs. Also, some of the functions mentioned by Russell show some kind of structural similarity.

In Chothe, the verb "be" can be divided into two categories, namely, copulative function of verb "be" and interrogative verb "be" form.

I. Copulative Function of Verb "be"

It is the linking verb. It links the subject to a complement. The sentence particle (SP) **-e~ye~we~ŋe~ke~ne,** etc. can be functioned as verb "be" in certain constructions. These SP are used as a copulative function of verb "be". It can be suffixed to proper noun, pronoun, identification, class membership, class inclusion, cardinal number and ordinal number.

A. Proper noun + "be"

Examples:-

6. (a) ləm-ha moyraŋ-ŋe
land-ddet. Moirang-be
'That land is Moirang.'

(b) ləm-hi ləndən-ne
land-pdet. London-be
'This land is London.'

B. Pronoun + "be"

Examples:-

7. (a) liŋlut-ha kə-ta-ye
shirt-ddet. pp-gen-be
'That shirt is mine.'

(b) tʰiŋ-pə-ha kəy-ye
go-NZ-ddet. I-be
'It is I who go there.'

C. Identification + "be"

Examples:-

8. (a) kəy dimho-we
I Dimho-be
'I am Dimho.'

(b) əmo wayren-ne
he Wairen-be
'He is Wairen.'

D. Class Membership + "be"

Examples:-

9. (a) mə-ŋəy ləwmi-ye
pp-pl. farmer-be
'They are farmer.'

(b) mə-ŋəy ilùpə-ye
pp-pl. thief-be
'They are thieves.'

E. Class Inclussion + "be"

Examples:-

10. (a) ət^{h}im-ha əpa-ye
doctor-ddet. man-be
'That doctor is a man.'

(b) ət^{h}im-ha numəy-ye
doctor-ddet. woman-be
'That doctor is a woman.'

F. Cardinal Number + "be"

Examples:-

11. (a) mə-ŋəy unaw-sənaw rəŋa-ye
pp-pl. sibling five-be
'They are five sibling.'

(b) mə-ŋəy mi inli-ye
pp-pl. man four-be
'They are four persons.'

G. Ordinal + "be"

Examples:-

12. (a) əpa-te-ha-nə inthum-su-pə-ye
man-small-ddet.-nom. three-comp.-NZ-be
'That boy is the third one.'

(b) numəy-te-ha-nə inli-su-pə-ye
woman-small-ddet.-nom. four-comp.-NZ-be
'That girl is the fourth one.'

II. Interrogative Verb "be" Forms

Chothe has interrogative verb "be" forms. The question marker **-mo** is used in yes/no question and the question marker **-me** is used in wh-question.

Yes-no question marker **-mo** can be suffixed to the noun and pronoun; it performs as a verb "be" as given in (13a-b).

Examples:-

13. (a) ha-na-ha uy-mo
ddet-away-ddet dog-Q.mk.
'Is that a dog?'

(b) əjan wa-pʰuy-pə-ha nəŋ-mo
Yesterday come-PER.asp.-NZ-ddet you-Q.mk.
'Are you the person who came yesterday?'

In the above examples, the question marker **-mo** is suffixed to the noun, namely, **uy** "dog" (i.e. **uy-mo**) as in (13a) and pronoun, namely, **nəŋ** "you" (i.e. **nəŋ-mo**) as in (13b). Thus, the question marker -mo is formed as a interrogative verb **"be"**.

The question marker **-mo** can also be added to determiner **hinahi** "this" and **hanaha** "that", etc. as given in the following sentences.

Examples:-

14. (a) əbay-ha hinahi-mo

book-ddet　　this-Q.mk.
'Is this the book?'

(b) uŋa-ha　　hanaha-mo
child-ddet　　that-Q.mk.
'Is that the child?'

In wh-question constructions, a different form is used, i.e. -**me** which is suffixed to wh-question words to perform the function of verb "be" as given below:-

ətu		who	
əropə		which	
ì		what	
ətuna		whose	
hoyke	+ me	where	+be
iyəŋŋə		why	
itikkə		when	
ərowa		how	

Thus, in Chothe, the verb "**be**" is used as a copulative function and interrogative verb "**be**" form.

Compound Verb

"Traditionally, a compound verb is supposed to exhibit functional unity. It contains one and only one "major verb" or pole. The vector is a "minor" verb in that it is (i) formally attached (it must occur immediately after the pole), (ii) semantically heteronomous (used as a vector, it does not have the autonomous meaning which it has in order sentences where it is used as a pole), (iii) grammatically subservient (it may not independently govern complements or modifier of it own). In contrast, a sequence of two poles contains, obviously, two poles rather than one. The second pole, even if morphologically similar to a vector, is (i) formally unattached (there may be elements between it and the first pole), (ii) semantically autonomous (carries its full lexical meaning), and (iii) grammatically central (it may govern complements or modifiers of its own)", (Dasgupta, 1989).

Examples of compound verbs are given from Hindi:-

(i) **a-ja** "come here" comes from **a-na** "to come" and **ja-na** "to go"

(ii) **beith-ja** "sit down" comes from **beith-ṇa** "to sit' and **ja-na** "to go"

Other examples from the "Aspect of HindiGrammar",(Kachru, 1980)

(a) Shîsha ṭûṭ gayâ
Mirror break went
'The mirror broke.'

(b) kapṛe dhul jâenge
cloth wash go will
'The cloth will be washed.'

In Bangala (Bengali) there occur verb plus verb constructions. It has been observed that verb plus particle constructions are often the best English renderings for Bangla compound verbs: thus, "sit down", "lie down" for **boSepOR** "sit and fall", **SuepOR** "lie and fall". Compound verbs are also found in non-Indo-European families such as Turkie, Tibeto-Burman, Japanese and Dravidian. Their use in Indo-Aryan, widespread in New Indo-Aryan times, goes back to the earliest phase of Middle Indo-Aryan, represented by Pali; (Dasgupta, 1989).

There are some compound verbs in Chothe. It may contain two verbal roots with the nominalizer **–pə**.

Examples:-

15. (a) bək-tʰiŋ-pə
eat-go-NZ
'go and eat'

(b) bək-wa-pə
eat-come-NZ
'eat and come'

(c) la-suk-pə
take-rise-NZ
'take off'

(d) in-wa-pə
drink-come-NZ
'drink and come'

In the sentence constructions, the nominalizer **–pə** is omitted from the compound verb. The sentence particle (SP) is suffixed to the compound verb.

Examples:-

16. (a) kəy bu bək-t^{h}iŋ-ŋe
I cook rice eat-go-SP
'I go and eat rice.'

(b) kəy bu bək-wa-we
I cook rice eat-come-SP
'I eat rice and come.'

The above examples, (16a) shows the action performed there, away from the speaker's place and (16b) shows the action is performed there and comes to inform the message to the speaker.

In Chothe, compound verbs also occur verb plus verb plus verb with the nominalizer **–pə**.

Examples:-

17. (a) la-suk-t^{h}iŋ-pə
go-rise-go-NZ
'go and take off'

(b) bək-suk-t^{h}iŋ-pə
eat-rise-go-NZ
'go and eat up'

The nominalizer **–pə** of the above compound verbs are also omitted in the sentence construction. The sentence particle (SP) is suffixed to the compound verbs.

Examples:-

18. (a) əmo-nə pəysa la-suk-t^{hl}iŋ-ŋe
he-nom money take-rise-go-SP
'He goes and takes off money.'

(b) kəy-nə bu bək-suk-t^{h}iŋ-ŋe
I-nom. cook rice eat-rise-go-SP
'I go and eat up rice.'

Tense or Aspect

The term "tense" derives (via old French) from the Latin translation of the Greek word for time (Greek **khronos**, Latin **tempus**). The category of tense has to do with time-relations in so far as these are expressed by systematic grammatical contrasts; (Lyons, 1968). Tense as category used in the grammatical description of verbs, refering primarily to the way the grammar marks the time at which the action denoted by the verb took place. In a very short and precise words of Comrie "Tense is grammaticalized expression of location in time" (Comrie, 1985). According to Hockett, "Tense typically shows different locations of an event in time: **John is eating a mango**, **John was eating a mango**. English verbs are inflected only for a two-way tense contrast, present and past; future time is expressed by other devices. This holds also in the other Germanic languages and in Slavic. A three way contrast is common: past, present and future (Hockett, 1958). But this three-way opposition of tense is not an universal feature of languages. In fact, tense is not found in all languages. "The essential characteristic is that it relates the time of action, event or state of affairs referred to the sentence to the time of utterance", (Lyons, 1968).

In Chothe, there is no grammatical time reference. "For grammaticalisation, it needs the interation between two parameters: that of obligatory expression, and that of morphological boundedness, whereas lexicalisation needs neither obligatory expression non morphological bounded-ness", (Comrie, 1985). It has temporal adverbials that locate situation in time such as:- **əjan** "yesterday", **uni** "today", **tutiŋ** "tomorrow", etc.

Examples:-

19. (a)

kəy	əjan	əsaŋ	tʰiŋ-ŋe
I	yesterday	Imphal	go-SP

'I went to Imphal yesterday.'
(I go to Imphal yesterday.)

(b)	kəy	uni	əsaŋ	t^hiŋ-ŋe
	I	today	Imphal	go-SP

'I go Imphal to-day.'

(c)	kəy	tutiŋ	əsaŋ	t^hiŋ- ŋəŋ-ŋe
	I	tomorrow	Imphal	go-pot.mk.-SP

'I shall go to Imphal to-morrow.'

The verb **t^hiŋ-ŋe** remains unchanged in the above sentence, as in (19a-b) and there is no addition or deletion of any element for denoting time reference. The time reference is indicated through the use of temporal adverbs:- **əjan** "yesterday" and **uni** "today" respectively in both the sentences. The verb **t^hiŋ -ŋəŋ-ŋe** "will go" as in (19c) is indicating an action not being performed, but having the possibility of being performed in the next moment (this is denoted by the potential marker -ŋəŋ), in another word -ŋəŋ indicates the futurity meaning.

The verb same form can be used with such temporal adverbs as **əjan** "yesterday", **tokni** "the day before yesterday", **uni** "today", **tutiŋ** "tomorrow", etc.

Examples:-.

20. (a)	əmo	əjan	əp^{h}əy	t^hiŋ-pə	di-ye
	he	yesterday	market	go-NZ	want-SP

'He wanted to go to the market, yesterday.'

(b)	əmo	tokni	əp^{h}əy	t^hiŋ-pə	di-ye
	he	day before yesterday	market	go-NZ	want-SP

'He wanted to go to the market, the day before yesterday.'

(c)	əmo	uni	əp^{h}əy	t^hiŋ-pə	di-ye
	he	to-day	market	go-NZ	want-SP

'He wants to go to the market, to-day.'

(d)	əmo	tutiŋ	əp^{h}əy	t^hiŋ-pə	di-ye
	he	tomorrow	market	go-NZ	want-SP

'He wants to go to the market, tomorrow.'

The same verb form **di-ye** is used with different temporal adverbs:- **əjan** "yesterday", **tokni** "the day before yesterday", **uni** "today" and **tutiŋ** "tomorrow" as in (20a-d) in the above examples.

In Chothe, there is no need of the interaction between the characteristic features of obligatory expression and that of morphological boundedness in the case of verbs, so it is concluded that there is no tense. There is no grammaticalized expression of location in time.

On the other hand, broadly the tense in Chothe can be classified into two systems i.e. future and non-future. Future will have future time reference in contrast with non-future which has no future time reference. They are given below:-

I. Non-future

The non-future tense is formed by **ø** morpheme with the sentence particle **-e~ye~we~ke~me~ne~le,** etc. They are suffixed to the verbal roots or stems.

Examples:-

21. (a) kəni ca in-ne
we tea drink-SP
'We drink tea.'

(b) əjan kəy sihom in-ne
yesterday I milk drink-SP
'Yesterday, I drink milk.'

(c) uni kəy sihom in-ne
today I milk drink-SP
'Today, I drink milk.'

(d) ətun kəy sihom in-ne
now I milk drink-SP
'Now, I drink milk.'

II. Future

Future tense is formed by adding the suffix **-əŋ~kəŋ~**

məŋ~nəŋ~ŋəŋ~yəŋ~wəŋ, etc. to the verbal roots or stems before the sentence particle. The suffix **-əŋ** occurs after the vowel phonemes and others occur after the consonant phonemes.

Examples:-

22. (a) kəy əsaŋ-ke wa-əŋ-ŋe
I Imphal come-F.mk.-SP
'I shall come to Imphal.'

(b) kəy sihom in-nəŋ-ŋe
I milk drink-F.mk.-SP
'I shall drink milk.'

The verb **in-ne** remains in all the sentences (21a-d) without even changing the suffix **-ne**. The meaning of the sentence (21a) is "We have the habit of drinking tea" or may be a simple statement that "We take tea". The same suffix **-ne** occurs with the adverbial time **əjan** "yearterday", **uni** "today' and **ətun** "now" as in the sentence (21b-d) respectively. But, in the case of future, the future marker-əŋ~**nəŋ**, etc. are suffixed to the verbal roots as in the sentence (22a-b).

Aspect

Aspect is concerned with the temporal distribution or contour of an event. In the words of Holt (Holt, 1943) "Aspects are different ways of viewing the internal temporal constituency of a sitution". In other words, it can be put in such a way that aspect indicates the internal structure of an event or situation. A well studied "Aspectual" contrast between perfective and imperfective is found in many Slavic languages: in Russia, for example, there is a perfective and imperfective contrast. For instance, the perfective form **onprocital** "he reads (something)", and the imperfective form **ončital** "he used to read/was reading (something)". The former refers to the completion of an action, while the later expressing duration without specifying completion.

Aspect is not concerned with relating the time of the situation to any other time-point, but rather with the internal temporal constituency of the one situation, one could state the difference as one between situation- internal time (aspect) and situation- external time (tense). Tense locates the event in time while aspect characterises the internal temporal structure of the event (Chung and Alan, 1985).

According to the Sino-Tibetanist, tense is not distinct in Tibeto-Burman languages. This indistinctiveness of tense is one of the structural features of TB languages. Bauman (Bauman, 1975) remarks that morphologically unmarked status of tense is a feature of TB. So, it would be more feasible to discuss of aspect in Chothe. It would be more convincing to say that there are four types of aspects. They are (i) Simple aspect (ii) Continous aspect (iii) Perfective aspect and (iv) Irrealis or unrrealised aspect. They are discussed below:-

I. Simple Aspect

In Chothe, simple aspect is formed by **ø** morpheme with the sentence particle (SP) **-e~ye~we~ke~me~ne~le,** etc. They are suffixed to the verbal roots or stems. It expresses simple statement or habitual meaning. The SP **-e~ye** occurs after the vowels except vowel /o/, the SP **-ye** also occurs after the approximant /y/.The SP **-we** occurs after the vowel /o/ and the approximant /w/. Others occur after the consonants which are lengthened.

Examples:-

23.	(a)	kəni	bu	bək-ke
		we	cook rice	eat-SP
		'We eat rice.'		
	(b)	kəy	əkəy	ən-ne
		I	tiger	look-SP
		'I look at a tiger.'		
	(c)	dimho	la	ŋay-ye
		Dimho	song	listen-SP
		'Dimho listens to a song.'		

(d) əmo　　t^{h}a-ye
he　　good-SP
'He is good.'

(e) nì-nə　　nəsu-ke　　suk-ke
sun-nom　　east-loc.　　rise-SP
'The sun rises in the east.'

II. Continous Aspect

The continous aspect is denoted by **-əm~kəm~məm~nəm~yəm,** etc. It is followed by the sentence particle **-me**. The suffix **-əm** occurs after the vowel phonemes and others occur after the consonant phonemes which are lengthened.

Examples:-

24. (a) kəy　　bu　　bək-kəm-me
I　　cook rice　　eat-CON.asp-SP
'I am eating rice.'

(b) t^{h}coŋ　　toŋ　　li-əm-me
Thachong　　speech　　speak-CON.asp-SP
'Thachong has been speaking.'

(c) əmo　　jay-yəm-me
he　　sleep-CON.asp-SP
'He is sleeping.'

III. Perfective Aspect

The perfective aspect markers are **-səw, -susəw** and **-p^{h}uy**. The event is only remote perfective, the aspect marker **-səw** occurs after the verbal roots or stems. The aspect marker **-phuy** occurs after the verbal roots or stems, when the event is more remote perfective. Then, the aspect marker **–susəw** occurs after the verbal roots or stems, when the event is perfective but completed before a while. The aspect markers **–səw** and **–susəw** are followed by the SP **-we** and the aspect marker **-p^{h}uy** is followed by the sentence particle (SP) **-ye**.

Examples:-

25.	(a) kəy	bu	bək-səw-we
	I	cook rice	eat-PER.asp-SP
	'I have taken rice.'(remote)		
	(b) kəy	əpʰəy	tʰiŋ-pʰuy-ye
	I	market	go-PER.asp.-SP
	'I have gone to market.'(more remote)		
	(c) kəy	bu	bək-susəw-we
	I	cook rice	eat-PERF.asp.-SP
	'I have taken rice.'(before a while)		

IV. Unrealised or Irrealis Aspect

It is used for the action which will take place in the near future. The suffix **-əŋ~kəŋ~ŋəŋ~yəŋ~məŋ**, etc. are used for the unrealised or irrealis aspect. The suffix **-əŋ** occurs after the vowel phonemes, the suffix **–yəŋ** and **–wəŋ** occur after the approximant /y/ and /w/ respectively. Other suffixes occur after the consonant phonemes. They are followed by the sentence final particle-**ŋe**.

Examples:-

26.	(a) kəy	iskul	tʰiŋ-ŋəŋ-ŋe
	I	school	go-UNR.asp.-SP
	'I will go to school.'		
	(b) əmo	bu	bək-kəŋ-ŋe
	he	cook rice	eat-UNR.asp.-SP
	'He will eat rice.'		
	(c) kəy	ìn-ke	wa-əŋ-ŋe
	I	house-loc.	come-UNR.asp.-SP
	'I will come at home.'		

From the above analysis, the non-future markers are same as the simple aspects. The non-future markers are not changed in relation to the adverbial of time **əjan** "yesterday", **uni** "today" and **ətun** "now" in the sentence (21b-d). So, there is no grammatical time reference, that is, there is no tence. Then, the future markers are also same as the unrealised or irrealis aspect. It shows that aspect seems more relevant than tense in Chothe. There are four aspect markers in Chothe. They are:- simple, continous, perfective and unrealised or irrealis aspects.

FIVE

Word Class

Noun

In Chothe, there are three classes of nouns on the basis of their structure, namely, (a) Simple nouns (b) Derived nouns and (c) Compound nouns.

Simple nouns are the single free roots and cannot be further divided into a simpler form, for instance; **uy** "dog", **si** "cow", **ok** "pig", **lu** "head", **ke** "leg", **saŋ** "paddy", etc.

Derived nouns are formed by affixation as exemplified below:-

1.	bək	'eat'	əbəkpə	'eater'
	in	'drink'	əinpə	'drinker'
	juy	'sale'	əjuypə	'saller'
	e	'do'	əepə	'doer', etc.

Compound nouns are the combination of two or more roots (see for detail in compounding).

Pronouns

Pronouns can be used to substitute for a noun phase (or a single noun). They can be subjects or objects of sentence. "We have so far treated the pronouns as a type of noun. This correctly reflects its major syntactic function, but it has special characteristics of its own" (Palmer, 1983). Personal pronouns have the plural suffix

-ni of their own. Demonstrative pronouns have the plural suffix -ŋəy. There are eight types of pronouns in Chothe. They are:- (i) Personal Pronouns, (ii) Possessive Pronouns, (iii) Demonstrative Pronouns, (iv) Interrogative Pronouns, (v) Indefinite Pronouns, (vi) Reflexive and Emphatic Pronouns, (vii) Reciprocal Pronouns and (viii) Pronoun of quantity.

I. Personal Pronouns

These pronouns are sub-divided into first, second and third persons. The first person refers to the speaker or speakers (e.g. **kəy** "I", and **əni** "we"). The second person refers to the person or persons spoken to (e.g. **nəŋ** "you"). The third person refers to the person or thing (people or things) spoken about (e.g. **əmo** "he", and **məni** "they"). The plural of the personal pronouns are indicated by the suffix **-ni** or **-ŋəy**.

The personal pronouns and possessive pronouns are shown in the following.

Person	**Number**	**Personal Pronouns**	**Possessive Pronouns**
First Person	Singular	kəy 'I'	kəta/kətəŋ 'mine' kəyta/kəytəŋ 'mine'
		Plural	kəni/əni 'we' ənita/ənitəŋ 'ours' kənita/kənitəŋ'ours'
Second Person	Singular	nəŋ 'you'	nəta/nətəŋ 'yours' nəŋta/nəŋtəŋ 'yours'
	Plural	nəŋəy/nəni 'you'	nənita/nənitəŋ 'yours' nəŋəyta/ nəŋəytəŋ'yours'
Third Person	Singular	əmo 'he/she/it'	məta/mətəŋ 'his/her/ its' əmota/əmotəŋ 'his/her/ its'
	Plural	məŋəy/məni 'they'	mənita/mənitəŋ 'their' məŋəyta/ məŋəytəŋ'theirs'

II. Possessive Pronouns

Possessive pronouns are formed through the suffixation of the genitive suffix **-ta** or **təŋ** to personal pronouns or pronominal prefixes. The suffix **-ta** is more familiar to the speaker of Chothe in the simple expression.

Examples:-

2. (a) pun-hi kə-ta-ye
   cloth-pdet pp-gen.-SP
   'This cloth is mine.'

   (b) pun-hi kə-ni-ta-ye
   cloth-pdet pp-pl-gen.-SP
   'This cloth is ours.'

   (c) pun-hi kəy-ta-ye
   cloth-pdet I-gen.-SP
   'This cloth is mine.'

In Chothe, the suffix **–təŋ** is used in the emphatic meaning.

Examples:-

3. (a) pun-hi kə-təŋ-ŋe
   cloth-pdet pp-gen.-SP
   'This cloth is mine.'

   (b) pun-hi kə-ni-təŋ-ŋe
   cloth-pdet pp-pl-gen.-SP
   'This cloth is ours.'

III. Demonstrative Pronouns

In Chothe, there are two demonstrative pronouns based on the two determiners (i.e. **-hi** "this" and **-ha** "that"). The two demonstrative pronouns are:- (a) **hinahi** "this and (b) **hanaha** "that (away from the speaker). They are composed of the determiner -**hi** or **-ha** and a particle **-na** denoting "away from the speaker".

Examples:-

4.	(a) hi-na-hi	kə-ta	pun-ne
	pdet-away-pdet	pp-gen	cloth-SP
	'This is my cloth.'		
	(b) ha-na-ha	nə-ta	əbay-ye
	ddet-away-ddet	pp-gen.	book-SP
	'That is your book.'		

The demonstrative pronouns can take the plural suffix **-ŋəy** and case suffixes. The plural suffix is followed by the suffix **-hi** or **-ha** and the case suffixes.

Examples:-

	Singular	**Plural**
5.	(a) hi-na-hi	hi-na-ŋəy-hi
	pdet-away-pdet	pdet-away-pl.-pdet
	'this'	'these'
	(b) ha-na-ha	ha-na-ŋəy-ha
	ddet-away-ddet	ddet-away-pl.-ddet
	'that'	'those'

Examples:-

6.	(a) hi-na-ŋəy-hi-nə	tulu-hi	e-mo
	pdet-away-pl-pdet-nom.	work-pdet	do-Q.mk.
	''Have these done this work.'		
	(b) ha-na-ŋəy-ha-nə	tulu-ha	e-mo
	ddet-away-pl-ddet-nom.	work-ddet	do-Q.mk.
	'Have those done that work.'		

IV. Interrogative Pronouns

These pronouns are used in asking questions. The interrogative pronouns are:- **i** "what" **ətu** "who" and **əropə** "which" consisting of the question marker-**me/-mo**.

Examples:-

7.	(a) ətu-nə	tulu-ha	e-me
	who-nom.	work-ddet	do-Q.mk.
	'Who did that work?'		

(b) ətu-nə tulu-hi e-mo
who-nom. work-pdet do-Q.mk.
'Who did this work?'

The plural suffix **-ŋəy** is added to the singular interrogative pronouns or reduplication the singular interrogative pronoun for the formation of the plurals and the question marker **-me** is added to the pronouns.

Examples:-

		Singular		**Plural**
8.	(a)	ətu-me who-Q.mk. 'who'		ətu-ŋəy-me Who-pl-Q.mk. ''who(pl)'
			or	ətu-ətu-me who-who-Q.mk. 'who (pl)'
			or	ətu-tu-me 'who(pl)'
	(b)	ì-me what-Q.mk. 'what'		ì-ŋəy-me what-pl-Q.mk. 'what(pl)'
			or	ì-ì-me what-what-Q.mk. 'What(pl)'
	(c)	əropə-me which-Q.mk. 'Which'		əropə-ŋəy-me which-pl-Q.mk. 'Which (pl)'
			or	əropə-əropə-me which-which-Q.mk. 'Which(pl)'
			or	əro-əropə-me 'Which'

The interrogative pronouns can co-occur with the plural suffix and the case suffix.

Examples:-

9. (a)

ətu -ŋəy-nə	bu-hi	bək-kəŋ-me
who-pl-nom.	cook rice-pdet	eat-pot.-Q.mk

'Who (pl) will eat this rice?'

(b)

ətu-ətu-nə	bu-hi	bək-kəŋ-me
who-who-nom	cook rice-pdet	eat-pot.-Q.mk.

'who (pl) will eat this rice?'

V. **Indefinite Pronouns**

The morphological structures of the indefinite pronouns are given below:-

10. (a) ətu-hoŋ-pə-ək^{h}a
who-like-NZ-one
'Someone'

(b) ətu-me-ək^{h}a
who-Q.mk.-one
'Someone'

(c) ətu-me-ətəy
who-Q.mk.-some
'Some person'

(d) ətu-kum
who-also
'Anybody/anybody also'

(e) ətu-ək^{h}a-cək
who-one-only
'Anybody'

11. (a) ì-me-ək^{h}a
what-Q.mk.-one
'Something'

(b) ì-kum
what-also
'Anything/anything also'

(c) ì-me-ətəy
what-Q.mk.-some
'Something'

(d) ì-ək^{h}a-cək
what-one-only
'Anything'

(e) ì-me-ək^{h}a-kum
what-Q.mk.-one-also
'Anything/anything also'

The indefinite pronouns, **ətu-hoŋ-pə-əkʰa, ətu-me-əkʰa** and **ətu-me-ətəy,** as in (10a-c), are used in affirmative sentences, whereas **ətu-kum** and **ətu-əkʰa-cək** are used in negative sentences. The indefinite pronouns, **ətu-hoŋ-pə-əkʰa** "someone" is used to mean one person who is not known to the speaker, whereas **ətu-me-əkʰa** "someone" is used to mean one person who is known to the speaker, but not disclosed to the hearer. And **ətu-me-ətəy** "some person" is used to mean either of the two meanings.

Examples:-

12.	(a)	ətu-hoŋ-pə-əkʰa	hina	wa-ye
		who-like-NZ-one	here	come-SP
		'Someone comes here.'		
	(b)	ətu-me-əkʰa	wa-ye	
		who-Q.mk.-one	come-SP	
		'Someone comes.'		
	(c)	ətu-me-ətəy	wa-ye	
		who-Q.mk.-some	come-SP	
		'Some persons come.'		

Then, the indefinite pronouns **ì-me-əkʰa, ì-me-ətəy** and **ì-me-əkʰa-kum** are used in affirmative sentences, whereas **ì-kum** and **ì-əkʰa-cək** are used in negative sentences.

Examples:-

13.	(a)	əmo-nə	ì-me-əkʰa	li-ye
		he-nom.	what-Q.mk.-one	say-SP
		'He said something.'		
	(b)	əmo-nə	ì-me-ətəy	li-ye
		he-nom.	what-Q.mk.-some	say-SP
		'He said something.'		
	(c)	əmo-nə	ì-me-əkʰa-kum	lon-wa-ye
		he-nom.	what-Q.mk.-one-also	bring-come-SP
		'He brings something also.'		

The indefinite pronouns **ətu-kum, ətu- əkʰa-cək, ì-kum** and **ì-(ə)kʰa-cək** are used in negative sentences.

Examples:-

14. (a) ətu-kum hina wa-no-we
who-also here come-neg.-SP
'None comes here.'

(b) ətu-əkʰa-cək wa-no-we
who-one-also come-neg.-SP
'Nobody comes.'

(c) əmo-nə ì-kum li-no-we
he-nom. what-also say-neg.-SP
'He said nothing.'

(d) kəy-nə ì-(ə)kʰa-cək bək-no-we
I-nom. what-one-only eat-neg.-SP
'I eat nothing.'

The nominative suffix **–nə** can be suffixed to **ətu-hoŋ-pə-əkʰa, ətu-me-əkʰa, ətu-əkʰa-cək, ətu-me-ətəy, ì-me-əkʰa** and **ì-me-ətəy.**

Examples:-

15. (a) ətu-me-ətəy-nə tulu-hi e-ye
who-Q.mk.-some-nom work-pdet do-SP
'Some persons do this work.'

(b) əmo-nə ì-me-əkʰa-nə dimho huk-ke
he-nom. what-Q.mk.-one-nom. Dimho beat-SP
'He beats Dimho by something.'

VI. Reflexive and Emphatic Pronoun

A reflexive pronoun is a pronoun that indicates that the object of the verb is co-referential with the subject (of the verb); in other words, the subject and the object of the verb relate to the same entity.

In Chothe, reflexive pronoun consists of a Personal Pronoun/ Pronominal Prefix followed by a bound root **mək** "self". The reflexive pronouns are **kə/kəy-mək** "myself", **əni/kəni-mək** "ourself", **nə/nəŋ-mək** "yourself", **nəŋəy/nəni-mək** "yourselves", **mə/əmo-mək** "himself/herself/itself" and **məni/ məŋəy-mək** "themselves". Their morphological structures are given in the following:-

	Singular	**Plural**
1st Person	kə/kəy-mək pp/I-self 'Myself'	kəni/əni-mək our/our-self 'Ourselves'
2nd Person	nə/nəŋ-mək pp/you-self 'Yourself'	nəni/nəŋəy-mək you (pl)-self 'Yourselves'
3rd Person	mə/əmo-mək pp/he or she or it-self 'himself or herself or itself'	məni/məŋəy-mək they-self 'themselves'

The formation of sentences with the reflexive pronouns are given below:-

Examples:-

16. (a) kəy-nə kəy-mək huk-ke
I-nom. I-self beat-SP
'I beat myself.'

(b) nəŋ-nə nəŋ-mək luŋsa-ye
you-nom. you-self scold-SP
'You scold yourself.'

(c) kə-ni-nə kə-ni-mək liŋləy-ye
pp-pl-nom. pp-pl-self love-SP
'We love ourselves.'

In Chothe, an emphatic pronoun is a pronoun emphasising the subject or object of a verb as a particular person or thing. An emphatic pronoun consists of a bound root **-pum** "body" is followed by the **–mək** "self". The emphatic pronouns are as follows with their morphological structures.

Examples:-

		Singular		**Plural**
17.	(a)	kə-pum-mək pp-body-self '(I) Myself'	(b)	kəni/əni-pum-mək we/we-body-self '(We) Ourselves'
	(c)	nə/nəŋ-pum-mək pp/you-body-self '(You)Yourself'	(d)	nəni/nəŋəy-pum-mək you(pl)/you(pl)-body-self '(You pl.) Yourselves'
	(e)	mə/əmo-pum-mək pp/he-body-self '(He) Himself/(She) Herself/(It)Itself'	(f)	məni/məŋəy-pum-mək they/they-body-self '(They)Themselves'

An emphatic pronoun can be the subject or object of a verb with or without the association of the pronoun or noun.

Examples:-

18. (a) kəy kə-pum-mək tulu-hi e-ye
I pp-body-self work-pdet do-SP
'I myself do this work.'

(b) kə-pum-mək tulu-hi e-ye
pp-body-self work-pdet do-SP
'I myself do this work.'

Both the above examples, as in (18a-b) are grammatical and acceptable. The emphatic pronoun **kəpummək** "I myself" occurs with the associated pronoun **kəy** "I' as the subject, as in (18a), whereas in (18b), the emphatic pronoun **kəpummək** "I myself" occurs as the subject without the associated pronoun **kəy**.

In Chothe, emphatic pronouns can take case suffixes. They are given below:-

Examples:-

19.	(a)	kəy-nə	pun-ha	mə-pum-mək-ke	pe-ye
		I-nom.	cloth-ddet	pp-body-self-loc.	give-SP
		'I give that cloth (he) himself.'			
	(b)	kəy-nə	liŋlut-hi	mə-pum-mək-ke	pe-ye
		I-nom.	shirt-pdet	pp-body-self-loc.	give-SP
		'I give this shirt (he) himself.'			

VII. Reciprocal Pronouns

The verb form which is composed of a verbal root followed by **-tʰakke** can express as a reciprocal meaning. The reciprocal pronoun **əkʰaritəkʰa** "with each other/ with one another" is used to make the reciprocal meaning. It shows a clear meaning of the verb form.

Examples:-

20.	(a)	kə-ni	əkʰa-rit	əkʰa	huk-tʰak-ke
		pp-pl	one-asso.	one	beat-rec.-SP
		'We beat with one another.'			
	(b)	nə-ŋəy	əkʰa-rit	əkʰa	li-tʰak-ke
		pp-pl	one-asso.	one	see-rec.-SP
		'You see with each other.'			

Without the reciprocal verb, the reciprocal pronoun alone can not express the reciprocal meaning.

Examples:-

21.	(a)*	kə-ni	əkʰa-rit	əkʰa	huk-ke
		pp-pl	one-asso.	one	beat-SP
		'We beat with one another.'			
	(b)	kə-ni	əkʰa-rit	əkʰa	huk-tʰak-ke
		pp-pl	one-asso	one	beat-rec.-SP
		'We beat with one another.'			

In the above examples, the sentence (21a) is ungrammatical and unacceptable because the reciprocal marker is not added but in the sentence (21b) is grammatical and acceptable, beacause the reciprocal marker is added to the verbal root.

Verbs

Verbs in this language are not a bound root. All the aspect markers are suffixed to the verb. There are three types of verb in this language i.e. (a) action verb (b) process verb and (c) stative verb (see for detail in verbal categories).

Adjectives

It is the main set of items which specify the attributes the nouns e.g. the **big** men, but it can occur in a post-verbal or "predicative" position, e.g. the man is **big**; then it can be premodified by an intensifier, such as **very**, e.g. the very **big** man; and it can be used in a comparative and superlative form either by inflection, e.g. **big, bigger, biggest** or periphrastically, e.g. **interesting, more interesting, most interesting.**

There are two important functions that adjectives are generally found to perform in natural languages. They are:-

(a) Restricting the scope of reference of a given noun to which the adjectives have been attached as an attribute in noun phrase:- **pun** "cloth", **pun əsənpə**"red cloth".

(b) Characterising the reference of a noun phrase with which the adjective has been used as a predicate in a sentence:- **mihi waŋŋe** "This man is tall".

The words functioning as adjectives from a distinct grammatical category in some language like English, whereas in others they are found to function as a sub-class of either (i) the nominal bases, or (ii) the verbal bases. In case of the Sanskrit language, adjectives function as nominal bases. They take number, gender and case terminations while occurring in the attributive as well as predicative positions. In fact, they do not even form a separate sub-class among the nominal bases of Sanskrit.

"Whereas the adjectives of Manipur function as verbal bases. They, along, with certain adverbial roots, constitute a sub-class of verbs, called statives, while occurring in the predicative position, they take tense, aspect, mood, voice and such other verbal affixes, whereas while occurring in the attributive position they take the infinitive suffix **-bə** and also, in some cases, the prefix ə-" (Bhat and Ningomba, 1986).

In Chothe, there are some adjectives which function as verbal bases and can occur in the predicative position. Some adjectives also occur in the attributive position (e.g. adjective denoting quality). They are discussed below:-

I. Adjective Denoting Quality

Adjective is derived from the verbal roots. In this case, Prefix ə- is used as a formative particle and nominalizer-pə is suffixed to the verbal root.

Examples:-

22. (a) ə-tʰ-pə mi
FP-good-NZ man
'Good man'

(b) ə-siŋ-pə mi
FP-wise-NZ man
'Wise man'

From the above examples (22a-b), the nominalizer **–pə** and the prefix **ə-** are affixed in the formation of adjectives in Chothe. There are some words which function as adjectives and which are derived from the action verbs or experiential verbs. In this case, there are two forms of adjectives.

I. One Form Consisting of the Formative Particle ə-.

Examples:-

23. (a) ju ə-in-pə mi
liquor FP-drink-NZ man
'Man (who) drink liquor'

(b) ə-dəŋ-pə mi
FP-know-NZ man
'Man (who) knows'

II. Other Form Which Does not Consist of the Formative Particle ə-

Examples:-

24. (a) i-pa
write-man
'Man writer'

(b) i-nu
write-woman
'Woman writer'

(c) siŋ-ləw-pə mi
wise-neg.-NZ man
'Unwise man

A different type of adjective formation has given the following phrases in different meanings.

Examples:-

25. (a) bək-kəŋ-pə bu
eat-pot-NZ cook rice
'Rice to be eaten' (by every man)

(b) kəy-nə bək-kəŋ-pə bu
I-nom. eat-pot-NZ cook rice
'Rice to be eaten by me'

(c) nəŋ-nə bək-kəŋ-pə bu
you-nom. eat-pot-NZ cook rice
'Rice to be eaten by you'

In Chothe, the distribution of adjectives denoting quality, can be noticed from its occurring in the attributive position, the adjectives precede the modified noun. While occurring after the modified nouns, they can take all the affixes.

Examples:-

26. (a) ə-t^ha-pə uŋa-ŋəy-hi-nə
FP-good-NZ child-pl-pdet-nom.
'These good children (noun)'

(b) uŋa ə-tʰa-pə-ŋəy-hi-nə
child FP-good-NZ-pl-pdet-nom.
'These good child (noun)'

In the above example (26a), **ə-tʰa-pə** "good" is an adjective denoting quality. It occurs before the noun. The suffix -ŋəy "plural", **-hi** "this" and **–nə** "nominative suffix" are directly suffixed after the noun **uŋa** "child". In the example (26b), the adjective occurs after the noun **uŋa** "child", the suffixes **-ŋəy** "plural", **-hi** "this" and **–nə** "nominative suffix"are directly suffixed after the adjective **ə-tʰa-pə** "good" (that is, **ə-tʰa-pə-ŋəy-hi-nə**).

II. Adjective Denoting Quantity

In Chothe, there are some words denoting quantity e.g. **ətəy** "some" and **ətəmpə/ ətəmmə** "much/many/very". These words are used as adjectives as well as adverbs and occur after the noun if it takes place as an adjective.

Examples:-

27. (a) mi ə-təy wa-ye
man FP-some come-SP
'Some men come.'

(b) mi ə-təmmə wa-ye
man FP-very come-SP
'Many men come.'

(c)* ə-təy mi wa-ye
FP-some man come-SP

In the above examples (27a-b), the adjectives occur after the modified noun, they are acceptable sentences. But the sentence (27c) is not acceptable because **ətəy** "some" occurs before the modified noun.

III. Adejectives Denoting Numerals

A. Cardinal Numbers

The numeral **əkʰa** "one", **əni** "two", **intʰum** "three", etc. are treated as nouns. They are used as adjectives when they modify nouns and occur after the nouns.

Examples:-

28. (a) əbay int^{h}um pe-wo
book three give-com.mk.
'(You,Sg.) Give three books.'

(b)* int^{h}um əbay pe-wo
three book give-com.mk.

In the above example, (28b) is unacceptable because the modified **int^{h}um** "three" occurs before the modified noun **əbay** "book", but the sentence (28a) is acceptable because the modifier **int^{h}um** "three" occurs after the modified noun.

B. Ordinal Number

The ordinal numbers:- **misapə** "first", **ənisupə** "second", **int^{h}umsupə** "third", etc. are used to modify nouns. They can occur before or after the modified nouns.

Examples:-

29. (a) misa-pə mi-ha kok-ko
first-NZ man-ddet call-com.mk.
'Call the first man.'

(b) mi əni-su-pə-ha kok-ko
man two-com.-NZ-ddet call-com.mk.
'Call the second man.'

III. Adejective Denoting Demontrative

In Chothe, demonstrative pronouns such as **hi** and **ha** etc. are also used as modifiers. They function as an adjective.

Examples:

30. (a) mi-hi
man-pdet
'This man'

(b) mi-ha
man-ddet
'That man'

(c) kolom-ŋəy-hi
pen-pl-pdet
'These pen'

(d) əbay-ŋəy-ha
book-pl-ddet
'Those book'

IV. Adjectives Denoting Possessors

In this form, the personal pronouns are used as possessors. It is different from the possessive pronoun morphologically. The possessive pronoun consists of the genetive suffix **-ta**. In the case of singular person, the pronominal prefix and suffix **-ta** are used as a possessor.

Examples:-

31. (a) kə-ta
pp-gen.
'Mine'

(b) nə-ta
pp-gen.
"Your's"

(c) kə-ta uy
pp-gen. dog
'My dog'

(d) kə-ta əbay
pp-gen. book
'My book'

(e) hi-na-hi kə-ta uy-ye
pdet-away-pdet pp-gen. dog-SP
'This is my dog.'

In the above examples, (31a-b) are possessive pronouns, whereas in the examples (31c-e) **kəta** is used as an adjective modifying the noun **uy** "dog" and **əbay** "book".

V. Adejectives of Comparison

In Chothe, there are three forms of comparison. They are:- (a) positive form (b) comparative form and (c) superlative form.

The positive form of adjective has no comparison. It express the adjective in the simple way.

Examples:-

32. (a) əmo ə-t^ha-pə numəy-ye
she FP-good-NZ woman-SP
'She is good woman.'

(b) hi-na-hi ə-ŋəw-pə pun-ne
pdet-away-pdet FP-white-NZ cloth-SP
'This is white cloth.'

The comparative form of an adjective is used for a comparison between two entities. It is marked with the suffix **-he** "er/more" and the nominalizer **–pə** to the adjectival (verbal) root.

Examples:-

33. (a) əmo-nə tombə-tre t^ha-he-pə əpate-ye
he-nom. Tomba-than good-er/more boy-SP
'He is better boy than Tomba.'

(b) t^hahoy-nə t^hanidəm-tre ənt^{h}a-he-pə numəyte-ye
Thahoi-nom. Thanidam-than beautiful-er/more NZ girl-SP
'Thahoi is more beautiful girl than Thanidam.'

(c) kəydi-nə mə-tre siŋ-he-pə uŋa-ye
Kaidi-nom pp-than wise-er/more-NZ child-SP
'Kaidi is wiser child than him.'

More examples of comparative form of the adjectives are given on the following page.

The superlative form of an adjective is used for a comparison between more than two entities. In this case, the suffix **-hetek** "est/most" and the nominalizer **–pə** are suffixed to the adjectival (verbal) root.

Examples:-

34. (a) t^ha-hetek-pə
good-est/most-NZ
'best'

(b) ŋəw-hetek-pə
white-est/most-NZ
'whitest'

Eamples in the sentence level:-

35. (a) əmo-nə t^ha-hetek-pə numəy-ye
He/she-nom. good-est/most-NZ woman-SP
'She is the best woman.'

(b) hi-na-hi ŋəw-hetek-pə liŋlut-te
pdet-away-pdet white-est/most-NZ shirt-SP
'This is the whitest cloth.'

More examples of comparative and superlative form of the adjectives are given in the following examples.

Adjective formation in Chothe

36.

Positive	**Comparative**	**Superlative**
ət^hapə 'good'	t^hahepə 'better'	t^hahetekpə 'best'
əsiŋpə 'wise'	siŋhepə 'wiser'	siŋhetekpə 'wisest'
əsənpə 'red'	sənhepə 'redder'	sənhetekpə 'reddest'
əsempə 'hot'	semhepə'hotter'	semhetekpə 'hottest'
ətoypə 'short'	toyhepə 'shorter'	toyhetekpə 'shortest'
əsəypə 'long'	səyhepə 'longer'	səyhetekpə 'longest'
ədikpə 'green'	dikhepə 'greener'	dikhetekpə 'greenest'
ədaypə 'cool'	dayhepə 'cooler'	dayhetekpə 'coolest'
əwaŋpə 'tall'	waŋhepə 'taller'	waŋhetekpə 'tallest'

In Chothe, the suffix **-he** "er/more" and the suffix **-hetek** "est/most" are the comparative and superlative forms of adjectives. Such formations of adjectives are not found in Manipuri. But Aimol has comparative and superlative form (Shamungou, 1995). The suffix **-det** "er/more" and **–tək** "est/most" are the comparative and superlative forms. In Ao, "the degrees of comparison are marked morphologically on the adjectives by adding the suffixes **-pa** and **-tipa** to indicate the comparative and superlative degrees respectively", (Gurubasave, 1975).

Adverbs

In Chothe, adverbs are derived from the verbal roots through the affixation of the suffixes **–yə~tə~mə~wə~nə,** etc. The suffix **–yə** occurs after the vowels and approximant /y/, the suffix **–wə** occurs after the approximant /w/ and others occur after the consonants which are lengthened. The suffix **–heyə** "-er/more" and **–hetekkə** "est/most" are used for comparison of adverbs.

Examples:-

37.	tət^{h}i-yə	tət^{h}i-heyə	tət^{h}i-hetekkə
	'nicely'	'more nicely'	'most nicely'
	not-tə	not-heyə	not-hetekkə
	'quickly'	'more quickly'	'most quickly'
	sum-mə	sum-heyə	sum-hetekkə
	'slowly'	'more slowly'	'most slowly'
	hərəw-wə	hərəw-heyə	hərəw-hetekkə
	'happily'	'more happily'	'most happily'
	tom-mə	tom-heyə	tom-hetekkə
	'cheaply'	'more cheaply'	'most cheaply'
	siŋ-ŋə	siŋ-heyə	siŋ-hetekkə
	'wisely'	'more wisely'	'most wisely'

There are some words which can be used as adjectives or as intensifier.

Examples:-

38. (a) əmo ətəm-mə t^{h}a-ye
he very-adv.mk. good-SP
'He is very good.'

(b) mi ətəm-mə wa-ye
man many-adv.mk. come-SP
'Many people (men) come.'

The word **ətəmmə** "very", as in (38a), is used as an intensifier and indicates the degree of **t^{h}a-ye** "good" whereas the word **ətəmmə**, as in (38b) functions as an adjective modifying the **mi** "man" indicating the plurality "many".

There are some words which function as temporal adverbs without the adverbial suffixes. They are:- **ətun** "now", **uni** "today", **əjan** "yesterday", **tutiŋ** "tomorrow", **nəkùm** "last year", **mət^{h}əŋkùm** "next year", etc.

The words **hinake**"here" and **hanake** "there" are used as locative adverbs.

Classification of Adverbs

In Chothe, adverbs can be classified into eight classes on the basis of their meanings. They are :- (i) Adverbs of manner (ii) Adverbs of place (iii) Adverbs of time (iv) Interrogative adverbs (v) Adverbs of order (vi) Adverbs of degree (vii) Adverbs of number and (viii) Adverbs of affirmation.

I. Adverbs of Manner

Adverbs of manner denote how an action is performed or how an event takes place. They are derived from adjectival (verbal) roots through the suffix **–tə~mə~yə~ŋə~nə**, etc.

Examples:-

39. (a) not-tə
quick-adv.mk.
'quickly'

(b) sum-mə
slow-adv.mk.
'slowly'

(b) tət^h^i-yə
nice-adv.mk.
'nicely'

(d) siŋ-ŋə
wise-adv.mk.
'wisely'

Examples in the sentence level:-

40. (a)

əmo	not-tə	t^h^iŋ-ŋe
he	quick-adv.mk.	go-SP

'He goes quickly.'

(b)

əmo	yaŋ-ŋə	tan-ne
he	first-adv.mk.	run-SP

'He runs firstly.'

From the above examples (40a), **not-tə** "quickly" functions as a adverb modifying the verb **t^h^iŋ-ŋe** "go + SP" and denotes how the action is performed (i.e. quickly), **not-tə** is derived from the adjectival (verbal) root **not** "quick" through the suffixation of **tə**. Then, in the sentence (40b) the word **yaŋ-ŋə** functions as an adverb modifying the verb **tan-ne** "run + SP" derived from **yaŋ** "quick" through the suffixation of the adverbal marker **-ŋə**.

II. Adverbs of Place

The adverbs **hinake** "here" and **hanake** "there" are treated as adverbs of place.

Examples:-

41. (a)

nəŋ	hinake	wa-o
you	here	come-com.mk.

'You come here.'

(b)

nəŋ	hanake	t^hiŋ-ŋo
you	there	go-com.mk.

'You go there.'

Then, the locative maker **-ke** and the ablative marker **-kena** are suffixed to a place. It can function as an adverb of place.

Examples:-

42. (a)

əmo	əsaŋ-ke	əm-me
he	Imphal-loc.	live-SP

'He lives at Imphal.'

(b)

əmo	əsaŋ-kena	wa-ye
he	Imphal-abl.	come-SP

'He comes from Imphal.'

III. Adverbs of Time

The adverbs of time in Chothe are **uni** "today", **əjan** "yesterday", **tutiŋ** "tomcrrow", **ətun** "now", **nəkùm** "last year", **mət^həŋkùm** "next year", etc. The names of days, months and years take the locative suffix **-ke/-keyə.** They can function as temporal adverbs.

Examples:-

43. (a)

uni	əmo	wa-əŋ-ŋe
today	he	come-UNR.asp-SP

'Today he will come.'

(b)

əsuni-keyə	əmo	wa-əŋ-ŋe
Saterday-loc.	he	come-UNR.asp-SP

'On Saturday he will come.'

(c)	əmo	puŋ	əret-ke	wa-əŋ-ŋe
	he	hour/o'clock	eight-loc	come-UNR.asp.-SP

'He will come at 8 o'clock.'

In the above examples (43a), **uni** "today" modifies the verb **wa-əŋ-ŋe** "will come", **əsuni-keyə** "on Saterday" modifies the verb **wa-əŋ-ŋe** "will come",as in (43b) and **puŋ əret-ke** "at 8 O'clock" modifies the verb **wa-əŋ-ŋe** "will come" as in (43c).

Temporal adverbs can be classified into three types in Chothe. They are (i) Point of time (ii) Extent or duration of the event or the state, and (iii) Goal or source of a given event or state.

A. Pont of Time

The point of time of a given event or state can be indicated by taking the locative suffix **-ke/-keyə**. The locative suffix **-ke/-keyə** is suffixed to the word **kəsuŋ/p^h^əw** "in/ within", **nuŋtiŋ** "after", **əma** "before", etc.

Examples:-

44.	(a)	əmo	puŋ	əret-ke	iskul	tʰiŋ-ŋəŋ-ŋe
		he	O'clock	eight-loc	school	go-UNR.asp.-SP

'He will go to school at 8 O'clock.'

(b)	kəy	puŋ	əku-ta	əma-ke	iskul	tʰiŋ-ŋəŋ-ŋe
	I	O' clock	nine-gen	before-loc	school	go-UNR. asp.-SP

'I will go to school before 9 O'clock.'

(c)	kəy	puŋ	əsom-ta	nuŋtiŋ-ke	iskul	tʰiŋ-ŋəŋ-ŋe
	I	O' clock	ten-gen	after-loc	school	go-UNR. asp.-SP

'I will go to school after 10 O'clock.'

B. Extent or Duration

In Chothe, the temporal adverbs can indicate extent or duration of the event or state. It does not take any suffixes.

Examples:-

45. (a)

kəy	puŋ	əsom	jay-ye
I	hour	ten	sleep-SP

'I sleep for ten hours.'

(b)

kùm	rəŋa	əsaŋ-ke	əm-me
year	five	Imphal-loc.	live-SP

'I have lived in Imphal for five years.'

(c)

kəy	puŋ	əni	oŋ-ŋe
I	hour	two	sit-SP

'I sit for two hours.'

C. Goal or Source

In Chothe, the nouns denoting time with the locative suffixes **–p^həwwə** "upto" and **-kena** "from/since" can function as a temporal adverbs indicating goal or source of the event or state.

Examples:-

46. (a)

puŋ	əret-p^həwwə	kəy	jay-ye
O'clock	eight-upto	I	sleep-SP

'I sleep upto eight O'clock.'

(b)

puŋ	əret-kena	kəy	jay-ye
O'clock	eight-since	I	sleep-SP

'I have been sleep since eight O'clock.'

There are other temporal adverbs such as **tokni** "day before yesterday" **əjan** "yesterday" **toknirəy** "some days back" **nitiyə** "everyday" and **əci** "before a while", etc.

IV. Interrogative Adverbs

The words **hoyke/ike** "where", **ijenə/iyenə/iyəŋŋə** "why", **ikena/hoykena** "from where", **ərowa/irowa** "how", **itikkə/iropəkankeyə** "when", etc. are used as interrogative adverbs.

Examples:-

47. (a) ike tʰiŋ-ŋəm-me
where go-CON.asp-Q.mk.
'Where are you going?'

(b) ərowa e-əm-me
how do-CON.asp-Q.mk.
'How are you doing?'

(c) iropəkankeyə bək-kəŋ-ŋe
when eat-UNR.asp-Q.mk.
'When will you eat?'

V. Adverbs of Order

It is derived from the ordinal numbers through the affixation of the suffix **-ke** in Chothe.

Examples:-

48. (a) misa-pə-ke
first-NZ-loc.
'in the first'

(b) əni-su-pə-ke
two-comp.-NZ-loc
'in the second'

(c) intʰum-su-pə-ke əmo wa-ye
three-comp.-NZ-loc he come-SP
'He comes in the third.'

VI. Adverbs of Degree

In Chothe, this kind of adverbs denotes the degree or quality. It answers the question "How much?" or "to what degree?". For instance, **ətəy** "some", **ətəmmə** "much/many", **təməy** "very", etc.

Examples:-

49. (a) əmo ətəy tʰa-ye
he some good-SP
'He is little good.'

(b) əmo təməy tʰa-ye
he very good-SP
'He is very good.'

(c) mi ətəmmə wa-ye
man many come-SP
'Many men come.'

VII. Adverbs of Number

It is derived through the process of compounding of **woy** "left side" + cardinal number + **rət/lət** "number of times". It shows the number of times in which an action is performed.

Examples:-

50. (a) woy-k^ha-rət
left-one-times
'once'

(b) woy-ni-rət
left-two-times
'twice'

(c) əmo woy-li-rət t^hiŋ-ŋe
he left-four-times go-SP
'He goes four times.'

VIII. Adverbs of Affirmation

The words **suynowə** "surely", **ət^{h}iŋŋə** "really" and **ədiktəkkə** "exactly" are used as adverbs of affirmation.

Examples:-

51. (a) əmo suynowə wa-ye
he surely come-SP
'He comes surely.'

(b) əmo ədiktəkkə dəŋ-ŋe
he exactly know-SP
'He knows exactly.'

Connectives

The words which join the clauses, phrases or words are treated as connectives. It can be classified into two categories :- (i) Co-ordinators (Co-ordinating conjunctions) and (ii) subordinators (subordinating conjunctions).

Co-ordinators are linking linguistic units of equivalent syntactic status e.g. a series of clauses or phrases or words. Co-ordinate clauses are illustrated in the sentence **John came and Mary left**: the marker of linkage is **and**, a co-ordinating conjunction (or Co-ordinator).

Subordinators are also linking linguistic units so that they have different syntactic status, one being dependent upon the other, and usually a constituent of the other. For instance, **John came when Mary left**; the marker of linkage is **when**, a subordinating conjunction (or subordinator). They are discussed below:-

A. Co-ordinators

In Chothe, co-ordinators are:- (i) **hatawettə** "and then" (ii) **hatəyəwk^{h}əy** "but" (iii) **hananə/hinanə** "therefore/so" (iv) **anore** "or" and (v) **ək^{h}akum** "and". These co-ordinators are discussed in the following.

I. hatawettə "and then"

It is used as addition of a syntactic status.

Examples:-

52. (a)

bu	bək-ko	hatawettə	iskul	t^{h}iŋ-ŋo
rice	eat-com.mk.	and then	school	go-com.mk.

'(You, Sg) Eat rice and then go to school.'

(b)

təkbuy-wo	hatawettə	bu	kəm-mo
bath-com.mk.	and then	rice	cook-com.mk.

'(You, Sg.) Take bath and then cook the rice.'

II. hatəyəwk^{h}əy "but"

It is used as a "contrast between two ideas".

Examples:-

53. (a)

əmo	t^{h}a-ye	hatəyəwk^{h}əy	coŋte	t^{h}a-no-we
he	good-SP	but	Chongte	good-neg.-SP

'He is good but Chongte is not good."

(b) kəy pun su-əŋ-ŋe hatəyəwk^{h}əy əmo pun su-əŋ-no-we
I cloth wash-UNR but he cloth wash-UNR.
asp.-SP asp-neg.-SP
'I will wash cloth, but he will not wash cloth.'

III. hananə/hinanə "therefore/so"

It is used in the meaning of "inference"

Examples:-

54. (a) əmo ju in-ne hananə kəy əmo-tə di-no-we
he liquor drink-SP therefore I he-acc. like-neg.-SP
'He drinks liquor, therefore I don't like him.'

(b) kəy bu bək-no-ye hinanə kəy iskul t^{h}iŋ-ŋəŋ-no-we
I rice eat-neg-SP therefore I school go-UNR.asp.-neg.SP
'I don't eat rice, therefore I will not go to school.'

IV. anore "or"

It gives the meaning of "choice" or "alternative".

Examples:-

55. (a) bək-ko anore in-no
eat-com.mk. or drink-com.mk.
'(You, Sg) Eat or drink.'

(b) nəŋ anore əmo wa-o
you or he come-com.mk.
'Come here (you, Sg or he).'

V. ək^{h}akum "and"

It is used in the sense of "adding" in Chothe.

Examples:-

56. (a) bək-ko ək^{h}akum in-no
eat-com.mk. and drink-com.mk.
'Eat and drink.'

(b)	əmo-tə	kok-ko	əkʰakum	əbay	pa-pi-o
	he-acc.	call-com.mk.	and	book	read-Hon.mk.-com.mk.

'Call him and read the book.'

B. Subordinating Conjunctions

There are verbal suffixes which are added to verbs of the clauses to form subordinate adverbial clauses. The suffixes are:- **wettə, -suwettə, -rille, -make, -pʰəwwə, -ləyyə, -kanke, -kena, -lecu/-recu, -lekum/-rekum,** etc. These suffixes can be divided into five types. They are:- (i) Suffixes denoting time (ii) Suffixes denoting cause (iii) Sufixes denoting condition (iv) Suffixes denoting concession and (v) Suffixes denoting comparison. They are discussed in the following.

I. Suffixes Denoting Time

In Chothe, suffixes such as **–wettə, -suwettə, -rille, -make, -pʰəwwə, -leyyə, -kanke** are added to verbs of the clauses to form subordinate adverbial clauses indicating time. They are given below:-

-wettə "after"

Examples:-

57.	(a)	əmo	wa-wettə	təkbuy-ye	
		he	come-after	bath-SP	

'After he comes he takes bath.'

	(b)	əmo	bək-wettə	pun	su-ye
		he	eat-after	cloth	wash-SP

'After he has eaten, he washes (cloth).'

-suwettə "remote complete"

Examples:-

58.	(a)	là	sa-su-wettə	kəy	wa-ye
		song	sing-finish-after	I	come-SP

'After I have sung (song), I come.'

(b) bu bək-su-wettə kəy tʰiŋ-ŋe
cook rice eat-finish-after I go-SP
'After I have eaten (rice), I go.'

-rille "immediately after/as soon as"

Examples:-

59. (a) kəy pəysa pʰa-rille kəy sinema ən-ne
I money get-immediately after I cinema look-SP

'As soon as I get money, I see a picture.'

(b) kəy pəysa pʰa-rille kəy liŋlut-ha ləy-ye
I money get-immediately after I shirt-ddet buy-SP
'As soon as I get money, I buy that shirt.'

-make "before"

Examples:-

60. (a) nəŋ bək-no-make wa-o
you eat-neg-before come-com.mk.
'(You, Sg) Come (here) before you eat.'

(b) nəŋ tʰiŋ-no-make bək-ko
you go-neg-before eat-com.mk.
'(You, Sg) Eat before you go.'

In the above examples (60a-b), **-make** is suffixed to the verb of the clause to form a subordinate adverbial clause. It denotes that the action of the main verb occurs first before the action denoted by the subordinate verb occurs.

-pʰəwwə "until"

Examples:-

61. (a) kəy wa-pʰəwwə hak-ko
I come-until wait-com.mk.
'(You, Sg) Wait until I come.'

	(b)	kəy	pəysa	p^{h}a-p^{h}əwwə	hak-ko
		I	money	get-until	wait-com.mk.

'(You, Sg) Wait until I get money.'

-ləyyə "during"

Examples:-

62.	(a)	kəy	əm-ləyyə	wa-o
		I	live-during	come-com.mk.

'While I am (here), (You,Sg) come.'

	(b)	kəy	əm-ləyyə	t^{h}iŋ-ŋo
		I	live-during	go-com.mk.

'While I am (here), (You, Sg) go.'

-kanke "when"

Examples:-

63.	(a)	əmo	t^{h}iŋ-kanke	pot-hi	pe-o
		he	go-when	thing-pdet	give-com.mk.

'When he goes, give this thing (to him).'

	(b)	kəy	wa-kanke	əmo	hinahi	əm-me
		I	come-when	he	here	live-SP

'When I come here, he lives here.'

II. Suffixes Denoting Cause

In Chothe, **-kena** is used as suffix denoting "cause". When it is added to the verb, the clause becomes subordinate clause.

-kena "as/because of/since"

Examples:-

64.	(a)	kəy	na-kena	bu	bək-no-we
		I	ill-as	cook rice	eat-neg.-SP

'As I am ill, I do not eat rice.'

	(b)	əmo-nə coy-kena	əbay-hi	tit-səw-we
		he-nom. hold-since	book-pdet	tear-PER.asp.-SP

'Since he holds, this book has been torn.'

III. Suffixes Denoting Condition

In Chothe, **-recu/-lecu** is suffixed to the verb, it becomes a subordinate adverbial clause, indicating "condition".

-recu/-lecu "if'

Examples:-

65. (a) nəŋ tʰiŋ-lecu kəy tʰiŋ-ŋəŋ-ŋe
you go-if I go-UNR.asp.-SP
'If you go, I shall go.'

(b) əmo wa-recu kəy tʰiŋ-ŋəŋ-ŋe
he come-if I go-UNR.asp.-SP
'If he comes, I shall go.'

IV. Suffixes Denoting Concession

The suffix **-rekum/-lekum** is used as a subordinating adverbial clause when it is suffixed to the verbal roots.

-rekum/-lekum "although"

Examples:-

66. (a) əmo bu bək-lekum ə-on puy-no-ye
he rice eat-although pp-belly swell-neg.-SP
'Though he eats rice, his belly does not swell.'

(b) əmo əbay pa-rekum i-kum dəŋ-no-we
he book read-although what-also know-neg-SP
'Though he reads books, he doesn't know anything.'

V. Suffix Denoting Comparison

In Chothe, the suffix **-tre** is added to the pronominal prefix or noun or pronoun or verb and the clause consisting of it becomes a subordinate adverbial clause.

-tre "than"

Examples:-

67. (a) kəy-nə mə-tre heyə bək-ke
I-nom. pp-than more eat-SP
'I eat more than him.'

(b) kəy-nə t^hanidəm-tre heyə waŋ-ŋe
I-nom. Thanidam-than more tall-SP
'I am taller than Thanidam.'

In Chothe, the word **tapə** is used as a quotative which joins a subordinate noun clause to an independent clause, when the embedded clause comes first the main clause occurs to its right.

Examples:-

68. (a) əmo t^ha-ye tapə kəy dəŋ-ŋe
he good-SP that I know-SP
'I know that he is good.'

(b) əmo t^ha-ye tapə-ha kəy dəŋ-ŋe
he good-SP that-ddet I know-SP
'I know that he is good.'

Interjection

It is a class of words which semantically express strong emotion and which do not enter into syntactic relationship with other classes

Interjection

o^h	"How can that be!"(expressing sadness/wonder of wonders)
o	"Oh"
ba	"Bravo!"
is	"How awful"
ha^h	"Surprise"
e	"Sorry"
əs	"How strange"
e^h	"Remember"
he	"How evil"
t^hacəw t^hacəw	"Well well"

Examples:-

69. (a) o^h! əmo t^hi-səw-we

wonderful he die-PER.asp.-SP

'Wonderful! he has died.'

(b) o! kənita cupipa hoŋpa wa-ye

oh our teacher Hongpa come-SP

'Oh! Our Sir, Hongpa comes.'

(c) ha^h! hina ì-me

surprise it what-Q.mk.

'Hah! What is this?'

(d) e! iyacək pəŋ-yəw-me

sorry how much fool-emph-Q.mk.

'What a fool (you) are!'

In Chothe, verbs (of statements) ending in suffix **-ehe/-è** function as interjections.

Examples:-

70. tɯy-è

tasty-interjection

'It is tasty.'

SIX

Word Formation and Lexical Rules

Word Formation

Word formation deals with "the creation of new words". It is the process of morphological variation in the contitution of words. It has two main divisions, viz, inflection and derivation. Derivation is divided into two branches, that is, affixation and compounding. Then, the compounding is divided into three types, that is, endocentric compound, exocentric compound and co-ordinate compound. Endocentric compound has two sub-types, that is, right headed compound and left headed compound.

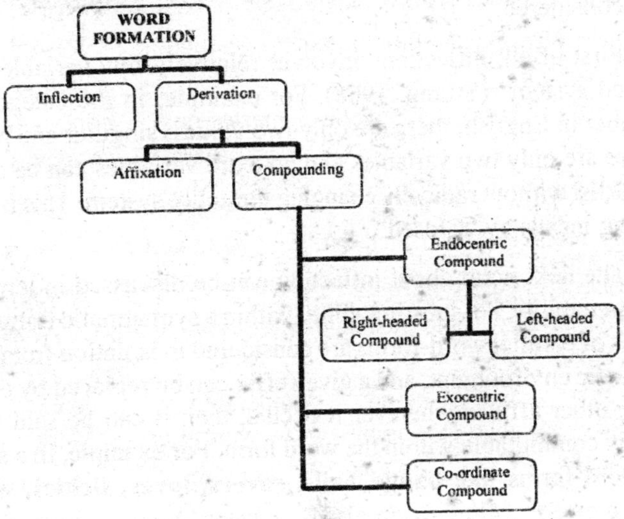

Inflection is the grammatical relationship such as plural, past tense and possession and does not change the grammatical class of the stems to which they are attached; that is, the words constitute a single paradigm e.g. walk, walks, walked. A word is said to "inflect for" past tense, plural etc. A particular bound morph expressing an inflectional distinction. For example, one can speak of the English plural suffix **-s** or the past tense suffix **-ed** as an inflection. Inflectional suffixes do not allow further suffixation. Inflectional suffixes are "terminal" and their terminal never changes the class (word class) of the root, for example, in **sweeter** and **sweetest**, the termination of **-er** by **-est** does not change the word class; both the forms remain adjectives.

"Inflection produces from the stem (or stems) of a given lexeme all the word-forms of that lexeme which occur in syntactically determined environments;" (Bauer, 1983).

This definition delimits, those processes which are inflectional, but, depending on how the lexeme is defined, it either runs the risk of circularity or, at best demands the inflection and lexeme are defined interdependently. The risk of circularity can be avoided, however, when all the characteristics of inflectional morphology are considered.

First of all, inflection "involves relatively few variables in a closed system" (Strang, 1968). For example, in the category of number in English, there are only two values: singular and plural. There are only two variables and no extra variables can be added to the list without radically changing the entire system. This is what Strang means by "Closed".

The next point about inflection can be discussed in terms of commutability, i.e. substitutability within a syntagmatic frame. If a series of parallel word-forms are considered in isolation from their syntactic environment, and a given affix can be replaced by one or more other affixes wherever it occurs, then it can be said to be highly commutable within the word form. For example, in a series of word forms like **bangs, calls, covers, loves, tickles, walks** the {s} is commutable with {ø}(= 'present tense, but not 3rd person singular'), {ing} and{ed}, but not with {let} and {ish}, through these affixes can be added to some of the bases.

Derivation is the morphological process that results in the formation of new lexemes (Lyons, 1977). It involves, or may involve, many variables in an open class (Strang, 1968). It is characterised by low commutability within the word-form, but a few kinds of derivation are characterised by high commutability within the sentence (feminine forms in **-ess** in English, diminutives and augmentatives in Italian, for examples). It is divided into two i.e. affixation and compounding.

Affixation is the process of attaching an affix to a root, base or stem. Affixes are of three types- prefix, infix and suffix. In English words such as **receive, remove, deceive, perform, unfaithful, unemployment,** the affix **re-, de-, un-** are all prefixes. The prefixes are affixed before the roots, stems or bases and cannot occur independently; they are bound morphemes. The plural formative **-s, -en**; the verb paradigm affixes **-ing, -ed** etc. the comparative and superlative ending of the adjectives **(-er** and **-est)** and so many final position formatives such as **-ness, -less, -ment** are called suffixes. Infixes are less commonly found in English apart from one mode of analysis of plurals like **geese, men.** Infixes are found in Cambodian, in Sudanese and in Sankrit too.

Compounding is the process of combining two or more existing words. For instance, **blackbird** from the element **black + bird,** and **newspaper** from the element **news + paper,** etc.

There are other proceses of word formation. These include - conversions, reduplication, clippings, acronyms, blends, borrowing, inventions, echoism, etc.

In Chothe, word-formation employs two processes i.e. (i) affixation and (ii) Compounding. The former process is paringly and later is used extensively and it is more productive. In this language, the pronominal prefixes **kə-, nə-** and **ə-/mə-** are found (see "Affixes"). In the present analysis infix is not included, because it is not found in this language. There are many suffixes in this language (see case suffixes, tense or aspect suffixes and verbal suffixes). In the word-formation of Chothe, the two processes take an important role.

Of these several ways of word formation, the derivational processes (i.e. affixation and compounding) will be discussed here. In Chothe, derived nouns can be formed by affixation and compounding.

Affixation

Noun can be derived from the verbal roots through the process of affixation. The derivational suffixes are:- (i) **–nəmun** (ii) **-pa** (iii) **-nu** (iv) **–pə** and (v) **-hi/-ha.**

I. –nəmun

The suffix **–nəmun** is added to the verbal roots to derive a noun.

Examples:-

		[Verbal root + nəmun]	>	Noun
1.	(a)	əm + nəmun live	>	əmnəmun 'address"
	(b)	naytʰuk + nəmun escape	>	naytʰuknəmun 'way of escaping'
	(c)	jay + nəmun sleep	>	jaynəmun 'place for sleeping'
	(d)	lut + nəmun enter	>	lutnəmun 'entrance'

II. -pa, -nu and –pə

Noun derived through the suffixation of **-pa** denote male human beings, whereas those derived through the suffixation of **-nu** denotes female (human beings). The suffix **–pə** denotes male or female human beings. It functions as a nominalizer. It can be represented in the following way:-

[ə + verbal root] + pa/nu/pə > Noun

Examples:-

2.	(a)	ə + hut + pa FP write M	>	əhutpa 'male writer'
	(b)	ə + hut + nu FP write F	>	əhutnu 'female writer'
	(c)	ə + hut + pə FP write NZ	>	əhutpə 'male/female writer'

III. Determiners -hi or -ha As Derivational Suffixes

Nouns can be derived from the modifier through the suffixation of the determiners. It can be represented in the following ways:-

[ə + Verbal root + pə] + hi/ha > Noun

Examples:-

3.	(a)	ə + bək + pə + hi FP eat NZ pdet	>	əbəkpəhi 'this one that eats'
	(b)	ə + bək + pə + ha FP eat NZ ddet	>	əbəkpə ha 'that one that eats'
	(c)	ə + wet + pə + hi FP mad NZ pdet	>	əwetpəhi 'this one that is mad'
	(d)	ə + wet + pə + ha FP mad NZ ddet	>	əwetpəha 'that one that is mad'

Compounding

It is composed of elements that function independently in other circumstances. They are consisting of two or more free morphemes, as in such "compound nouns" as **bedroom, postman, matchbox,** etc.

"The compound words occurring in a language can be studied either from the point of view of their own structure (for example, the kind of constituent elements that occur in them, or the function that these elements are found to carry out in the establishment of composite words) or from the point of view of their underlying structures." (Bhat and Ningomba, 1968).

For instance, in Chothe, **ŋarry** "ell fish" is a compound noun and the underlying structure can be established like this- a type of fish, the head of which is like a snake and so on.

There are three types of compounding. They are (i) endocentric compounds (ii) exocentric compounds and (iii) co-ordinate compounds.

Endocentric Compounds

Endocentric compounds consist of two elements. It always consists of attribute or subordinate and head or centre. For intence, **mitmùy** "eyelash" is an endocentric compound consisting of two elements, namely, **mit** "eye" **mùy** "body hair". In this compound **mùy** "lash" functions as the head and **mit** "eye" functions as the attribute of **mùy.**

There are two main types of endocentric compounds. They are (i) right-headed compounds and (ii) left-headed compounds.

I. Right-Headed Compounds

In the right-headed compounds, the second element is the head, whereas the first element is the attribute. In Chothe, right-headed compounds may be (a) noun + noun and (b) noun + derived noun as in the following.

(A) Noun + noun

Examples:-

4. (a) əwa + muy > əwamuy
   bird mouth 'beak of a bird'

   (b) mit + mùy > mitmùy
   eye body hair 'eyelash'

   (c) əru + əbu > əruəbu
   bamboo leaf 'leaf of bamboo'

(d)	mənsu + əbu		>	mənsuəbu
	sugarcane leaf			'leaf of sugarcane'

(B) Noun + Derived Noun

Examples:-

5. (a)	ìn	+ sapa	>	ìnsapa
	house	make(M)		'house maker (M)'
(b)	la	+ hoŋnu	>	lahoŋnu
	thread	make (F)		'weaver (F)'
(c)	bu	+ kəmpa	>	bukəmpa
	rice	cook (M)		'cook man'
(d)	pun	+ sunu	>	punsunu
	cloth	wash (F)		'washer (F)'
(e)	ərun	+ supa	>	əruŋsupa
	stone	work (M)		'mason (M)'

There are some compound nouns. They are composed of a noun + a verbal root and a derivational suffix –**nəmun.**

Examples:-

[Noun + Verbal root + nəmun] > Compound Noun

6. (a)	nì + suk + nəmun	>	nìsuknəmun
	sun rise		'place where sun rises'
(b)	nì + ta + nəmun	>	nìtanəmun
	sun fall		'place where sun enter'

In the underlying structures, the constituent elements of right-headed compounds may be two types:- (i) possessive relation and (ii) Verbal relation. They are discussed below:-

1. Possessive Relation

In Chothe, the possessive relation is denoted through the prefixation of the pronominal prefix ə- to the second element (noun). In this case, the formation of compound nouns, the pronominal prefix is deleted.

Examples:-

		Compound Nouns	**Underlying Structures**	
7.	(a)	t^{h}iŋbu	t^{h}iŋ	ə-bu
		leaf (of a tree)	wood	pp-leaf
			'leaf of a tree'	
	(b)	keme	ke	ə-me
		'foot-print'	leg	pp-back/behind
			'back of leg'	
	(c)	əwamùy	əwa	ə-mùy
		'beak (of a bird)'	bird	pp-mouth
			'beak of a bird'	
	(d)	k^{h}utjay	k^{h}ut	ə-jay
		'middle finger'	hand	pp-middle
			'middle of hand'	
	(e)	mitcuŋ	mit	ə-cuŋ
		'centre of eye'	eye	pp-centre
			'centre of eye'	
	(f)	mitt^{h}uy	mit	ə-t^{h}uy
		'below of eye'	eye	pp-below
			'below of eye'	
	(g)	mitmuy	mit	ə-muy
		'eyelash'	eye	pp-body hair
			'hair of eye'	
	(h)	mithəw	mit	ə-həw
		'eyelid'	eye	pp-border
			'border of eye'	

2. Verbal Relation

In Chothe, the two constituent elements of right-headed compound nouns may be related with each other by verbal relation in the underlying structures.

Examples:-

		Compound Nouns	Underlying Structures		
8.	(a)	ləmuy	ləm-ke	əm-pə	uy
		'fox'	wild-loc.	live-NZ	dog
			'dog which lives in wild'		
	(b)	ləmaytok	ləm-ke	əm-pə	aytok
		'wildduck'	wild-loc.	live-NZ	duck
			'duck which lives in wild'		
	(c)	ìnəsa	ìn-ke	əm-pə	ə-sa
		'domestic animal'	house-loc.	live-NZ	att.-animal
			'animal which lives in house'		
	(d)	ləməsa	ləm-ke	əm-pə	ə-sa
		'wild animal'	wild-loc.	live-NZ	att.-animal
			'animal which lives in wild'		
	(e)	ənbe	ən	kəm-pə	be
		'curry pot'	curry	cook-NZ	pot
			'pot for cooking curry'		
	(f)	keləmpi	ke-nə	t^hiŋ-pə	ləmpi
		'foot-path'	leg-inst.	go-NZ	path
			'path, a place through which people go on foot'		

II. Left-headed Compounds

There are two elements in the left-headed compounds. The two elements may be nouns, or the first element is a noun whereas the second element is an adjective.

In the case of the left-headed compounds consisting of two elements which are nouns, the first element and the second element can be related with each other by an adjective in the underlying structure, but in the process of compounding the formative particle ə- may or may not be deleted in Chothe.

Examples:-

	Compound Nouns	**Underlying Structures**		
9.	(a) ŋaruy	ŋa	əruy	kayyə
	'eel fish'	fish	snake	look like
		'fish that looks like a snake'		
			or	
		əruy	kayyə	ŋa
		snake	look like	fish
		'fish that looks like a snake'		
	(b) t^{h}əwhuy	t^{h}əw	huy	kayyə
	'honey bee'	fly	bee	look like
		'fly that looks like a bee'		
			or	
		huy	kayyə	t^{h}əw
		bee	look like	fly
		'fly that looks like a bee'		
	(c) kopipay	kopi	əpay	kayyə
	'cauliflower'	cabbage	flower	look like
		'cabbage that looks like a flower'		
			or	
		əpay	kayyə	kopi
		flower	look like	cabbage
		'cabbage that looks like a flower'		
	(d) ŋaok	ŋa	ok	kayyə
	'lata fish'	fish	pig	look like
		'fish that looks like a pig'		
			or	
		ok	kayyə	ŋa
		pig	look like	fish
		'fish that looks like a pig'		

Further, in the case of left-headed compound where the first element is a noun and second element is an adjective, the first element and the second element can be related with each other by supplying the formative particle ə- and the nominalizer **–pə** which has been deleted in the process of compounding (in Chothe, an adjective is composed of a formative particle (FP) ə- and a verbal root with the nominalizer **–pə**).

Examples:-

	Compound Nouns	Underlying Structures	
10.	(a) misiŋ 'wise man'	mi man 'wise man'	ə-siŋ-pə FP-wise-NZ
	(b) kùmtʰəw 'new year'	kùm year 'New year'	ə-tʰəw-pə FP-new-NZ
	(c) mitop 'stranger'	mi man 'other man'	ə-top-pə FP-other-NZ
	(d) minim 'short man'	mi man 'short man'	ə-nim-pə FP-short-NZ
	(e) mirok 'big man'	mi man 'big man'	ə-rok-pə FP-big-NZ
	(f) misin 'small man'	mi man 'small man'	ə-sin-pə FP-small-NZ

Exocentric Compounds

It is a group of syntactically related words where none of the words are functionally equivalent to the group as a whole (i.e. there is no definable "Centre" or "Head" inside the group). In Chothe, exocentric compounds are generally made up of a noun or nouns and a verbal root. Both the noun and the verbal root cannot be regarded as a head or the attribute in these compounds. It shows to postulate a covert element as the head.

Examples:-

	Compound Nouns	Underlying Structures			
11.	(a) luəypə 'head ache'	lu head	əy-pə ache-NZ		ləyna disease
		'disease in which head aches'			
	(b) haəypə 'teeth ache'	ha teeth	əy-pə ache-NZ		ləyna disease
		'disease in which teeth aches'			
	(c) puməypə 'body ache'	pum body	əy-pə ache-NZ		ləyna disease
		'disease in which body aches'			
	(d) lumay haypə 'vertigo'	lu head	may face	hay-pə quiver -NZ	ləyna disease
		'disease in which head and face quiver'			

Coordinate Compounds

There are two elements in co-ordinate compounds. They contain neither head or attribute, but they are made up of two different nouns. In the underlying structures of co-ordinate compounds, the two elements can be related with each other by a connective such as **əkʰakum/əkʰacu** "and" in Chothe.

Examples:-

	Compound Nouns	Underlying Structures		
12.	(a) bu-ən 'rice and curry'	bu rice	əkʰakum corn.	ən curry
		'rice and curry'		
	(b) si-ok 'cow and pig'	si cow	əkʰakum corn.	ok pig
		'cow and pig'		

(c)	bube-ənbe	bube	ək^{h}akum	ənbe
	'rice pot and curry pot'	rice pot	corn.	curry-pot
		'rice pot and curry pot'		
(d)	cəm-səy	cəm	ək^{h}akum	səy
	'knife and spear'	knife	corn.	spear
		'knife and spear'		
(e)	aytu-ayhen	aytu	ək^{h}akum	ayhen
	'knowledge and magic'	knowledge	corn.	magic
		'knowledge and magic'		
(f)	əsa-əŋa	əsa	ək^{h}akum	əŋa
	'animal and fish'	animal	corn.	fish
		'animal and fish'		
(g)	kəp^{h}ut-kəplaŋ	kəp^{h}ut	ək^{h}akum	kəplaŋ
	'spring and steam'	spring	corn.	steam
		'spring and steam'		
(h)	may-mit	may	ək^{h}akum	mit
	'face and eye'	face	corn.	eye
		'face and eye'		
(i)	t^{h}iŋto-ləwto	t^{h}iŋto	ək^{h}akum	ləwto
	'tree and paddy plant'	tree	corn.	paddy plant
		'tree and paddy plant'		
(j)	buhu-bərəy	buhu	ək^{h}akum	bərəy
	'a shallow basket and winnowing fan'	a shall-ow basket	corn.	winno-wing-fan
		'a shallow basket and win nowing fan'		
(k)	b^{h}u-ənhu	b^{h}u	ək^{h}akum	ənhu
	'plate and bowl'	plate	corn.	bowl
		'plate and bowl'		

(l) saŋ-cisay	saŋ	ək^hakum	cisay
'paddy and rice'	paddy	corn.	rice
	'paddy and rice'		
(m) pun-ni	pun	ək^hakum	ni
'cloth and loin cloth'	cloth	corn.	loin cloth
	'cloth and loin cloth'		
(n) t^hiŋ-tuy	t^hiŋ	ək^hakum	tuy
'firewood and water'	firewood	corn.	water
	'firewood and water'		
(o) ke-k^hut	ke	ək^hakum	k^hut
'foot and hand'	foot	corn.	hand
	'foot and hand'		
(p) mit-nukuy	mit	ək^hakum	nukuy
'eye and ear'	eye	corn.	ear
	'eye and ear'		
(q) ìn-ləw	ìn	ək^hakum	ləw
'house and paddy plant'	house	corn.	paddy plant
	'house and paddy plant'		

Formation of Verbs

In Chothe, verb is formed by the suffixation of aspect markers to the verbal roots and occurs finally in a sentence with a sentence particle, (see for detail in 5.3 verbs).

Formation of Adjectives

In the formation of adjectives, prefix ə- is used as a formative particle and nominalizer **–pə** is suffixed to the verbal roots, (see for detail in 5.4 Adjectives).

Formation of Adverbs

Adverbs are formed by the suffixation of the marker **–yə~tə~mə~nə~kə**, etc. to the verbal roots, (see for detail in 5.5 Adverbs).

Lexical Rules

A rule which derives lexical entries from lexical entries. Lexical rules are found in the particular morphological environment is a limited number especially for the formation of adverbs in Chothe.

The adverbial marker **–wə** is affixed to the roots or stems ending vowel **/o/** and approximant **/w/.** Then the adverbial **–yə** is affixed to the roots or stems ending vowels**/i,e,a,u/** and approximant **/y/.** Other adverbial markers **-mə~tə~nə~mə~ŋə**,etc. are affixed to the roots or stems ending consonants which are lengthened.

I. Suffixation of –wə to The Vowel Ending /o/

Examples:-

13. (a) uyto + -wə > uyto-wə
   'luxury' luxury-adv.mk.
   'luxuriously'

(b) suy-no + -wə > suy-no-wə
   false-neg false-neg-adv.mk.
   'not false' 'not falsely'

(c) dero + -wə > dero-wə
   'bright' bright-adv.mk.
   'brightly'

II. Suffixation Of –wə to the Approximant Ending /w/

Examples:-

14. (a) hərəw + -wə > hərəw-wə
   'happy' happy-adv.mk.
   'happily'

(b) t^haraw + -wə > t^haraw-wə
   'wet' wet-adv.mk.
   'wetly'

III. Suffixation of –yə to the Vowel Ending /i,e,a,u/

Examples:-

15. (a)	təthi nice 'nice'	+	-yə	>	təthi-yə nice-adv.mk. 'nicely'
(b)	he 'excessive'	+	-yə	>	he-yə excessive-adv.mk. 'excessively'
(c)	tha 'good'	+	-yə	>	tha-yə good-adv.mk. 'well/good(adv.)'
(d)	əthu 'rotten'	+	-yə	>	əthu-yə 'rotten-adv.mk. 'rottenly'

IV. Suffixation of –yə to the Approximant Ending /y/

Examples:-

16. (a)	əsəy 'long'	+	-yə	>	əsəy-yə long-adv.mk. 'longly'
(b)	ətoy 'short'	+	-yə	>	ətoy-yə short-adv.mk. 'shortly'
(c)	ənoy 'fat'	+	-yə	>	ənoy-yə fat-adv.mk. 'fatly'

V. Suffixation of –mə to the Consonant Ending /m/

Examples:-

17. (a)	tom 'cheap'	+	-mə	>	tom-mə cheap-adv.mk. 'cheaply'
(b)	sum 'slow'	+	-mə	>	sum-mə slow-adv.mk.

(c) kum + -mə > kum-mə
'loose' loose-adv.mk.
'loosely'

VI. Suffixation of –tə to the Consonant Ending /t/

Examples:-

18. (a) ənot + -tə > ənot-tə
'quick' quick-adv.mk.
'quickly'

(b) ərat + -tə > ərat-tə
'hard' hard-adv.mk.
'hardly'

(c) siŋŋet + -tə > siŋŋet-tə
'care' care-adv.mk.
'carefully'

VII. Suffixation of –kə to the Consonant Ending /k/

Examples:-

19. (a) ərok + -kə > ərok-kə
'large' large-adv.mk.
'largely'

(b) ədik + -kə > ədik-kə
'fresh' fresh-adv.mk.
'freshly'

(c) əpek + -kə > əpek-kə
'wide' wide-adv.mk.
'widely'

VIII. Suffixation of -ŋə to the consonant Ending /ŋ/

Examples:-

20. (a) siŋ + -ŋə > siŋ-ŋə
'wise' wise-adv.mk.
'wisely'

	(b)	əjəŋ 'straight'	+	-ŋə	>	əjəŋ-ŋə straight-adv.mk. 'straightly'
	(c)	waŋ 'tall'	+	-ŋə	>	waŋ-ŋə tall-adv.mk. 'tall(adv.)'

IX. Suffixation of –nə to the Consonant Ending /n/

Examples:-

21.	(a)	əran 'false'	+	-nə	>	əran-nə false-adv.mk. 'falsely'
	(b)	əsən 'red'	+	-nə	>	əsən-nə red-adv.mk. 'redly'
	(c)	kən 'hard'	+	-nə	>	kən-nə hard-adv.mk. 'hardly'

SEVEN

Phrase and Clause

Phrase

A form consisting to two or more words is a phrase. "Any group of words which is grammatically equivalent to a simple word and which does not have its own subject and predicate is a phrase",(Lyons, 1968).

There are four types of phrase in Chothe. They are :- (i) Noun phrase (ii) Verb phrase (iii) Adjective phrase and (iv) Adverb phrase.

Noun Phrase

The construction into which nouns most commonly enter, and of which they are the head word, are generally called noun phrases (NP) or "nominal groups". The structure of a noun phrase consists minimally of the noun (or noun substitute, such as a pronoun); the other words or affixes can be added.

Examples:-

1. (a) uŋa-ha
   child-ddet
   'That child'

   (b) pun-hi
   cloth-pdet
   'This cloth'

   (c) əbay   pa-əm-pə   uŋa-ha
   book   read-live-NZ   child-ddet
   'The boy who read the book'

Verb Phrase

David Crystal (1985) remarked that "the term verb phrase is used in two senses. Traditionally, it refers to a group of verbs which together have the syntactic function as a single verb e.g. is coming, get up to. In such phrases, verbal groups, verbal cluster, one verb is the main verb (the lexical verb) and the others are subordinate to it (auxiliary verbs, catenative verbs). A verb followed by a non-verbal particle (similar in form to a preposition or adverb) is generally referred to as a phrasal verb.

In generative grammar, the verb phrase (VP) has a much broader definition, being equivalent to the whole of the predicate of a sentence, as is clear from the expansion of S as NP + VP in phrase-structure grammar.

In Chothe, VP consists of a verbal root, an adverb and a sentence particle.

Examples:-

2 (a) ətəm-mə bək-ke
very-adv.mk eat-SP
'eat very much'

(b) ətəm-mə tʰa-ye
very-adv.mk good-SP
'very good'

(c) yaŋ-ŋə tan-ne
fast-adv.mk. run-SP
'run fastly'

A verb-phrase may also be contained in the order of an adverb, a verbal root, an aspect marker and a sentence particle.

Examples:-

3. (a) ənot-tə tʰiŋ-səw-we
quick-adv.mk. go-PER.asp.-SP
'has gone quickly'

(b) sum-mə　　　　t^{h}iŋ-ŋəŋ-ŋe
slow-adv.mk.　　　go-UNR.asp.-SP
'will go slowly'

Adjective Phrase

A phrase which functions as an adjective is known as adjective phrase.

Examples:-

4. (a) ə-t^{h}a-pə　　　əpa-te
FP-good-NZ　　　man-small
'good boy'

(b) ə-siŋ-pə　　　əpa
FP-wise-NZ　　　man
'wise man'

(c) əjan　　　wa-pə
yesterday　　　come-NZ
'who came yesterday'

Adverb Phrase

Aphrase which functions as an adverb is known as adverb phrase.

Examples:-

5. (a) ətəm-mə　　　not-tə
very-adv.mk.　　　quick-adv.mk.
'very quickly'

(b) ətəm-mə　　　tət^{h}i-yə
very-adv.mk.　　　nice-adv.mk.
'very nicely'

(c) ətəm-mə　　　sum-mə
very-adv.mk.　　　slow-adv.mk.
'very slowly'

Clause

It is a group of words with its own subject and predicate, if it is included in a larger sentence. In traditional grammar, a clause is regarded as excluding any subordinate clauses embedded in it; in all contemporary work, however, such embedded clauses are considered to form part of the matrix clause.

TYPES OF CLAUSE

Clause may be divided into two types in Chothe. They are (i) independent clause and (ii) non-independent clause (dependent clause).

CLAUSE

Independent Clause — Dependent (Non-Independent) Clause

INDEPENDENT CLAUSE

A clause that functions as a sentence is known as independent clause.

Examples:-

6. (a)

əmo	dəŋ-ŋe
he	know-SP

'He knows.'

(b)

kəy	bu	bək-səw-we
I	rice	eat-PER.asp.-SP

'I have taken meal.'

(c)

əbay-ha	tʰa-ye
book-ddet	good-SP

'That book is good.'

DEPENDENT (NON-INDEPENDENT) CLAUSE

A clause that can not function as a sentence is known as non-independent (dependent) clause.

Examples:-

7. (a) əmo bu bək-kəŋ-no-we li-rekum bək-ke
he rice eat-pot-neg.-SP say-although eat-SP
'He says that he does not eat rice although he eats rice.'

(b) əmo dəŋ-no-we li-pə-ha cum-me
he know-neg.-SP say-NZ-ddet true-SP
'It is true that he does not know.'

(c) əmo bu bək-səw-we ha-na-wettə t^{h}iŋ-səw-we
he rice eat-PER.asp-SP ddet-away-after go-PER.asp-SP
'He has gone after eating.'

In the above examples, (7a) **li-rekum bək-ke** (7b) **li-pə-ha cum-me** and (7c) **ha-na-wettə t^{h}iŋ-səw-we** are the non-independent (dependent) clauses. They cannot function as a sentence.

STRUCTURE OF CLAUSE

On the structure of clause, sentence can be divided into three types. They are (i) Simple sentence, (ii) complex sentence and (iii) compound sentence.

SIMPLE SENTENCE

These sentences have one verb only in an independent clause. There is no verbal pronomonalization. The normal order of words in a sentence is SOV (Subject-Object-Verb) i.e. the verb is in the final position of the sentence.

Examples:-

8. (a) kəy tuy in-ne
I water drink-SP
'I drink water.'

(b) əmo iskul t^{h}iŋ-ŋe
he school go-SP
'He goes to school.'

(c) kəy nəŋ dəŋ-ŋe
I you know-SP
'I know you.'

In simple sentences, adverbs precede the verbs (see adverbs); the determiner **-hi/-ha** and plural suffix **-ŋəy** are suffixed to the nouns (see number); the numerals precede the verbs (see numerals); case markers are suffixed to the nouns (see case) and aspect markers are suffixed to the verbal roots (see tence or aspect).

OTHER EXAMPLES

9. (a) əmo ìn-keyə wa-ye
he house-loc. come-SP
'He comes at home.'

(b) əmo təkbuy-ye
he bath-SP
'He takes bath.'

(c) kəy bu bək-səw-we
I rice eat-PER.asp-SP
'I have taken meal.'

(d) əmo iskul tʰiŋ-ŋəŋ-ŋe
he school go-UNR.asp-SP
'He will go to school.'

COMPLEX SENTENCE

A complex sentence sonsists of at least a matrix clause and one or more dependent clauses. In Chothe, it may be constructed by suffixing a nominalizer **–pə** to the verb.

Examples:-

10. (a) əmo-nə hoŋ-pə pun-ha əntʰa-ye
he-nom. weave-NZ cloth-ddet nice-SP
'The cloth which he weave is nice.'

(b) kəy-nə lon-wa-pə uy-ha maŋ-səw-we
I-nom. carry-come-NZ dog-ddet lose-PER.asp-SP
'The dog which I brought has been lost.'

In the above examples, (10a) **pun-ha əntʰa-ye** "that cloth is nice" and (10b) **uy-ha maŋ-səw-we** "the dog has been lost" are matrix clause; then in (10a) **əmo-nə hoŋ-pə** and (10b) **kəy-nə lon-wa-pə** are the dependent clause.

The example (10a) can be written into two independent clauses is given below:-

11. (i) əmo-nə pun-ha hoŋ-ŋe
    he-nom. cloth-ddet weave-SP
    'He weaves that cloth.'

    (ii) pun-ha əntʰa-ye
    cloth-ddet nice-SP
    'That cloth is nice.'

The above two independent clauses (11i) and (11 ii) make up a complex sentence (10a) with the help of the nominalizer **–pə** which is suffixed to the verb **hoŋ** "weave".

Regarding the sentence (10b) can also be written as two independent clauses as given in the following:-

12. (i) kəy-nə uy-ha lon-wa-ye
    I-nom. dog-ddet carry-come-SP
    'I bring that dog.'

    (ii) uy-ha maŋ-səw-we
    dog-ddet lose-PER.asp.-SP
    'That dog has been lost.'

The above two independent clauses (12i) and (12 ii) form a complex sentence (10b) with the help of the niminalizer **–pə** which is suffixed to the verb **lon-wa** "bring".

In Chothe, complex sentences are also formed with the help of verbal suffixes:- **-wettə** "after", **-suwettə** "remote complete", **-rille** "as soon as" **-make** "before", **-pʰəwwə** "until" **-ləyyə** "during", **-kanke** "when", **-kena** "as/because of/since", **-lecu/-recu** "if", **-rekum/-lekum** "although", etc. (see the examples of subordinating conjunction). With the help of these verbal suffixes are suffixed to the verbal roots or stems as a connector of the dependent clauses and independent clauses to make the complex sentences.

In Chothe, Complex sentences may contain more than one dependent clause and are multiple embedding.

Examples:-

13. (a)

əmo-nə	lon-wa-pə	tebəl-keyə	əm-pə	əbay-ha	t^{h}a-ye
he-nom.	carry-come-NZ	table-loc.	live-NZ	book-ddet	good-SP

'The book which is on the table and which you bring is good.'

(b)

kəy-nə	in-pə	əmo-nə	lon-wa-pə	ju-ha	tuy-ye
I-nom.	drink-NZ	he-nom.	carry-come-NZ	liquor-ddet	tasty-SP

'The liquor that I drink and which you bring is tasty.'

In the above examples, (13a-b), there are two dependent clauses in each sentence. The nominalizer –**pə** connect the two dependent clauses with the independent clause. In the example (13a), **əmo-nə lon-wa-pə** and **tebəl-keyə əm-pə** are the dependent clauses; and **əbay-ha t^{h}a-ye** is the independent clause. In the example (13b), **kəy-nə in-pə** and **əmo-nə lon-wa-pə** are the dependent clauses; and **ju-ha tuy-ye** is the independent clause. They are connected with the nominalizer –**pə**. The above example, (13a) can be written into three independent clauses are given in the following:-

Examples:-

14. (i)

əmo-nə	əbay-ha	lon-wa-ye
he-nom.	book-ddet	carry-come-SP

'He brings that book.'

(ii)

tebəl-keyə	əbay-ha	əm-me
table-loc.	book-ddet	live-SP

'That book is on the table.'

(iii)	əbay-ha	t^ha-ye
	book-ddet	good-SP

'That book is good.'

The above three independent clauses (14i), (14ii) and (14iii) form the complex sentence (13a) with the help of the nominalizer **–pə**. In the same way, the complex sentence (13b) can be written into three independent clauses. They can form a complex sentence with the help of the nominalizer-**pə**.

COMPOUND SENTENCE

In Chothe, Compound sentences contain at least two independent clauses and are normally connected by a coordinating conjunction. But all the compound sentences are not necessarily to be connected by a connector. So the compound sentences may be divided into two types:- (a) Compound sentences having a connective and (b) Compound sentences without a connective.

A. COMPOUND SENTENCES HAVING A CONNECTIVE

There are five types of connectives used in these types of sentences. They are:- **hananə/hinanə** "therefore/so", **hatəyəwk^{h}əy** "but", **anore** "or", **hatawettə** "and then" and **ək^{h}akum** "and".

Examples:-

15.(a)	əmo ju	in-ne	hananə	kəy	əmo-tə	di-no-we
	he liquor	drink-SP	therefore	I	he-acc.	like-neg.-SP

'He drinks liquor therefore I don't like him.'

(b)	əmo	t^ha-ye	hatəyəwk^{h}əy	nəŋ	t^ha-no-we
	he	good-SP	but	you	good-neg.-SP

'He is good but you are not good.'

(c)	nəŋ	hi-na-hi	wa-o	anore	əmo-tə	kok-ko
	you	pdet-away-pdet	come-com.mk.	or	he-acc.	call-com.mk.

'You come here or you call him.'

(d)	nəŋ	əpʰəy	tʰiŋ-ŋo	hatawettə	liŋlut	juy-yo
	you	market	go-com.mk.	and then	shirt	buy-com.mk.

'You go to market and then buy a shirt.'

(e)	əmo	kok-ko	əkʰakum	əbay	pa-pi-o
	he	call-com-mk.	and	book	read-Hon.mk.-com.mk.

'Call him and read the book.'

B. COMPOUND SENTENCES (WITHOUT CONNECTIVE) / (WITH A COORDINATE CONSTRUCTION)

These types of sentences are an overt coordinate construction with a juxtaposed asyndetically. They may be four types of sentence constructions. They are:- (i) Statement + Statement (ii) Statement + Interrogative (iii) Statement + Imperative and (iv) Imperative + Imperative, etc.

I. STATEMENT + STATEMENT

It has two independent clauses (of simple statements) of an overt coordinate construction with a juxtaposed asyndetically.

Examples:-

16. (a)	kəy	ju	misa-a	in-nəŋ-ŋe	me	luynuŋ-ŋə	bək-kəŋ-ŋe
	I	liquor	first	drink-UNR. asp.-SP	meat	later-adv. mk	eat-UNR. asp.-SP

'I will drink liquor first, I will eat meat later.'

(b)	kəy-nə	əbay	pa-e	əmo-nə	lakʰa-pə	tʰiŋ-ŋe
	I-nom.	book	read-SP	he-nom.	play-NZ	go-SP

'I read the book, he goes to play.'

II. STATEMENT + INTERROGATIVE

It has two independent clauses (of a simple statement and an interrogative) of an overt coordinate construction with a juxtaposed asyndetically.

Examples:-

17. (a)

kəy	hu-keyə	tʰiŋ-ŋəŋ-ŋe	nəŋ	tʰiŋ-ŋəŋ-mo
I	village-loc.	go-UNR.asp-SP	you	go-UNR.asp.-Q.mk.

'I will go to the village, will you go?'

(b)

kəni	ju	in-nəŋ-ŋe	nəŋ	in-nəŋ-mo
we	liquor	drink-UNR.asp-SP	you	drink-UNR.asp-Q.mk.

'We will drink liquor, will you drink?'

III. STATEMENT + IMPERATIVE

There are two independent clauses (of a simple statement and an imperative) of an overt coordinate construction with a juxtaposed asyndetically.

Examples:-

18. (a)

kəy	me	bək-kəŋ-ŋe	nəŋ-kum	bək-ko
I	meat	eat-UNR.asp-SP	you-also	eat-com.mk.

'I will eat meat, you also eat.'

(b)

kəy	iskul	tʰiŋ-ŋəŋ-ŋe	nəŋ-kum	tʰiŋ-ŋo
I	school	go-UNR.asp.-SP	you-also	go-com.mk.

'I will go to school, you also go.'

IV. IMPERATIVE + IMPERATIVE

There are two independent clauses (of two imperatives) of an overt coordinate construction with a juxtaposed asyndetically.

Examples:-

19. (a)

nəŋ	wa-o	tulu-hi	e-o
you	come-com.mk	work-pdet	do-com.mk.

'Come, do this work.'

(b)

nəŋ	tʰiŋ-ŋo	bu	bək-tʰiŋ-ŋo
you	go-com.mk.	cook rice	eat-go-com.mk.

'Go, eat the rice.'

EIGHT

SYNTACTIVIZATION

RELATIVIZATION

It is the process of forming a relative clause construction. In Chothe, there are two main types of clauses for carrying out the function of relative clauses i.e. the modification of nouns through sentence. They are:- (i) External relative clauses and (ii) Internal relative clauses. In both of these types of clauses, the sentence particle (SP) is changed into the nominalizer **–pə** of the verb.

I. EXTERNAL RELATIVE CLAUSE

In this type of relative clauses the noun (head noun) occurs outside the clause. The clause qualifies the noun in the attributive position.

Examples:-

1. (a) kəy-nə   əbay-ha   lon-wa-ye
   I-nom.   book-ddet   bring-come-SP
   'I bring the book.'

   (b) əbay-ha t^ha-ye
   book-ddet   good-SP
   'This book is good.'

   (c) kəy-nə   lon-wa-pə   əbay-ha t^ha-ye
   I-nom.   bring-come-NZ   book-ddet   good-SP
   'The book which I bring is good.'

In the above examples, the sentence (1c) is the external relative clause and is formed by embedding the sentence (1a) and (1b). The SP **-ye** of the sentence (1a) is deleted, intead of it a nominalizer **–pə** is suffixed to the verb to make the clause **kəy-nə lon-wa-pə** which qualifies the noun (head noun) **əbay-ha** "the book" in the attributive position. The noun (head noun) occurs outside the relative clause.

II. INTERNAL RELATIVE CLAUSE

In this type of relative clauses, the noun (head noun) occurs inside the clause. The clause qualifies the noun in the predicative position. Cole et al. (1982) refers to internal relatives as "headless relative" because the head (the NP that is being relativized) does not occur in the matrix clause, but only in the embedded sentence.

Examples:-

2. (a)

kəy-nə	uŋa-ha	huk-ke
I-nom.	child-ddet	beat-SP

'I beat the child.'

(b)

uŋa-ha	kəp-pəm-me
child-ddet	cry-CON.asp-SP

'The child is crying.'

(c)

kəy-nə	uŋa	huk-pə-ha	kəp-pəm-me
I-nom.	child	beat-NZ-ddet	cry-CON.asp-SP

'The child whom I beat is crying.'

In the above examples, the sentence (2c) is the internal relative clause. It is formed by embedding the sentence (2a) and (2b). The SP **-ke** of the sentence (2a) is deleted and a nominalizer **–pə** is suffixed to the verb and it is followed by the determiner **-ha**, to make the internal relative clause i.e. the sentence (2c). The noun (head noun) **uŋa** "child" is retained inside the clause without the determiner **-ha** i.e. the noun in the matrix clause has been deleted. It qualifies the noun in the predicative position.

NOMINALIZATION

Nominalizations are regarded as nouns derived from the verbs with the general meaning of an action or process having the capability of declining or taking prepositions or postpositions in the same way as non-derived nouns and showing "resonable" productivity. The Tibeto-Burman languages are highly nominalizing. In Chothe, even the stative verb can also be nominalized; the nominalizing suffix is highly productive and it occurs finally. All the action, process and stative are free roots and known as verbal roots. They can be nominalized by suffixation of the NZ –**pə**, as in the following two ways:- (i) addition to the direct roots and (ii) after the other suffixes.

I. ADDITION TO THE DIRECT ROOTS

(A) Action verbal roots

bək	+	pə	>	bək-pə	'to eat'
eat		NZ			
in	+	pə	>	in-pə	'to drink'
drink		NZ			
hut	+	pə	>	hut-pə	'to write'
write		NZ			
pe	+	pə	>	pe-pə	'to give'
give		NZ			

(B). Process Verbal Roots

taw	+	pə	>	taw-pə	'to float'
float		NZ			
min	+	pə	>	min-pə	'to ripe'
ripe		NZ			
ta/tuy	+	pə	>	ta/tuy-pə	'to fall'
fall		NZ			

yuŋ fly	+	pə NZ	>	yuŋ-pə	'to fly'
p^huy boil	+	pə NZ	>	p^huy-pə	'to boil'

(C). Stative Verbal Roots

day cold	+	pə NZ	>	day-pə	'to be cold'
rok big	+	pə NZ	>	rok-pə	'to be big'
sin small	+	pə NZ	>	sin-pə	'to be small'
rit heavy	+	pə NZ	>	rit-pə	'to be heavy'

II. AFTER THE OTHER SUFFIXES

In this case, the nominalizer **–pə** can be suffixed to the aspect markers (simple, continous/progressive, perfective and unrealized or irrealis) and the negative marker etc. They are discussed in detail in the followings.

Simple Aspect:- In Chothe, simple aspect marker is **ø**. The nominalizer **–pə** can be suffixed just after the verbal roots.

Examples:-

3. (a) bək > bək-pə 'to eat'
   eat

   (b) in > in-pə 'to drink'
   drink

4. (a) kəy bək-pə di-ye
   I eat-NZ like-SP
   'I like to eat.'

   (b) əmo in-pə t^hiŋ-ŋe
   he drink-NZ go-SP
   'He goes to drink.'

Continous/Progressive Aspect:- The nominalizer **–pə** can be added just after the continous aspect **-əm~kəm ~ŋəŋ~məm ~nəm~yəm,** etc. as in the following.

Examples:-

3. (a) bu bək-kəm-pə uŋa
rice eat-CON.asp-NZ child
'The eating child (the child who is eating)'

(b) t^hiŋ-ŋəm-pə mi
go-CON.asp.-NZ man
'The going person'

Perfective Aspect:-The nominalizer **–pə** can be suffixed just after the perfective aspect **–səw/-susəw/-p^huy** as given in the following examples.

5. (a) bək-səw + pə > bək-səw-pə
eat-PER.asp. NZ eat-PER.asp-NZ
'.....that is eaten (remote)'

(b) in-susəw + pə > in-susəw-pə
drink-PER.asp. NZ drink-PER.asp.-NZ
'....that is drunk (before a while)'

(c) in-p^huy + pə > in-p^huy-pə
drink-PER.asp. NZ drink-PER.asp.-NZ
'...that is drunk (more remote)'

(d) bək-səw-pə mi-ha
eat-PER.asp.-NZ man-ddet
'That man who has to eat.'

Unrealized or Irrealis Aspect:- It is also nominalizer **-pə** can be added just after the unrealized or Irrealis aspect **-əŋ~kəŋ ~ŋəŋ~məŋ~n̆əŋ,** etc.

Examples:-

6.	(a) bək-kəŋ	+ pə	>	bək-kəŋ-pə
	eat-UNR.asp.	NZ		eat-UNR.asp.-NZ
				'to be eaten'
	(b) in-nəŋ	+ pə	>	in-nəŋ-pə
	drink-UNR.asp.	NZ		drink-UNR.asp-NZ
				'to be drunk'

The nominalizer **–pə** can also be added to the negative marker **–ləw/-rəw** as given below:-

7.	(a) bək-ləw	+ pə	>	bək-ləw-pə
	eat-neg.	NZ		eat-neg.-NZ
				'not to eat'
	(b) in-ləw	+ pə	>	in-ləw-pə
	drink-neg.	NZ		drink-neg.-NZ
				'not to drink'
	(c) siŋ-ləw	+ pə	>	siŋ-ləw-pə
	wise-neg.	NZ		wise-neg.-NZ
				'unwise'
	(d) t^hiŋ-ləw	+ pə	>	t^hiŋ-ləw-pə
	go-neg.	NZ		go-neg.-NZ
				'not to go'

COMPLEMENTATION

It is the grammatical process of which sentences are formed to function as the argument of matrix sentence. Complement constructions are intricate and are varied in many natural languages. There are two different types of complementation in Chothe. They are:- (i) Complementation by Nominalization and (ii) Complementation by Nominalization with Determiner.

I. COMPLEMENTATION BY NOMINALIZATION

The nominalizer **–pə** is suffixed to a verb for the formation of nominal complement.

Examples:-

8. (a)

kəy	bək-pə	di-ye
I	eat-NZ	like-SP

'I like to eat.'

(b)

kəy	t^hiŋ-pə	di-ye
I	go-NZ	like-SP

'I like to go.'

In the above sentences, the nominalizer **–pə** is used for the formation of complement of the nounphrase (NP) **kəy bək-pə** 'I eat + NZ' and 'I go + NZ' respectively.

There are another type of nominal complement i.e. the matrix clause follows the complement.

Examples:-

9. (a)

tombə-nə	iskul	t^hiŋ-pə	kəy-nə	dəŋ-ŋe
Tomba-nom.	school	go-NZ	I-nom.	know-SP

'I know that Tomba goes to school.'

(b)

əmo	wa-pə	kəy-nə	dəŋ-ŋe
he	come-NZ	I-nom.	know-SP

'I know that he comes.'

And the complement is embedded into the matrix (that is between subject and predicate).

Example:-

10.

kəy-nə	tombə	iskul	t^hiŋ-pə	dəŋ-ŋe
I-nom.	Tomba	school	go-NZ	know-SP

'I know Tomba goes to school.'

II. COMPLIMENTATION BY NOMINALIZATION WITH DETERMINER

The nominalizer **–pə** and determiner **-ha** can be suffixed to the verb for making a complement sentence.

Examples:-

11. (a) əmo-nə tulu e-pə-ha kəy mək-ke
he-nom. work do-NZ-ddet I forget-SP
'I forget that he does the work.'

(b) tombə-nə liŋlut əkʰa la-pə-ha kəy-nə dəŋ-ŋe
Tomba-nom. shirt one take-NZ-ddet I-nom. know-SP
'I know that Tomba takes the shirt.'

REDUPLICATION

"A particular type of grammatical formation, whereby a part or the whole of a root is repeated in the same word is found in a number of languages to varying extents, that is known as reduplication and is describable either as a process or as an addition. In Malay, Sundanese and other Malaya Polynesian languages, the reduplication of entire word forms is a regular means of forming noun plurals (it also serves other grammatical purpose); thus

Malay	/kapal/	ship,	/kapal kapal/ ships;
Sundanese	/sirɣm/	ant,	/sirɣm sirɣm/ants.
			(Robins,1964)

Reduplications can be prefixes, infixes or suffixes.

In Tagalog language:-

sulat 'write' susulat 'will write'

In Mam language:-

toloŋ 'rol (a log)' tololoŋ 'water in rolling'

In Chothe, reduplication can occur in nouns, wh-question words, adverbs and verbs.

I. NOUNS

Examples:-

12. (a) in ınin
'house' 'respective houses/houses'

(b) simləy simləysimləy
'country' 'respective counries/countries'

(c) hu huhu
'village' 'respective villages/villages'

They occur in sentences.

Examples:-

13. (a)

kəni	inìn	cəŋon-ta	tʰiŋ-ŋe
we	houses	every-gen	go-SP

'We go to every house.'

(b)

məni	simləysimləy	cəŋon-ta	tʰiŋ-ŋe
they	countries	every-gen.	go-SP

'They go to every country.'

OTHER EXAMPLES

14. (a)	əni	'two'	əni əni	'two each'
(b)	inli	'four'	inli inli	'four each'
(c)	əret	'eight'	əret əret	'eight each'

They occur in the sentences.

15. (a)

kəni	lupa	inli inli	la-e
we	rupee	four four	take-SP

'We take Rs four each.'

(b)

məni	əbay	əni əni	juy-ye
they	book	two two	buy-SP

'They buy two books each.'

II. Wh-QUESTION

Examples:-

16. (a)	ətu-me	(b)	ətu-ətu-me
	who-Q.mk.		who-who-Q.mk.
	'Who'		'Who(pl)'

17.	(a)	ì-me what-Q.mk. 'What'	(b)	ì-ì-me what-what-Q.mk. 'What(pl)'
18.	(a)	iropə-me which-Q.mk. 'Which'	(b)	iro-iropə-me which-which-Q.mk. 'Which(pl)'
19.	(a)	hoyke-me where-Q.mk. 'Where'	(b)	hoyke-hoyke-me where-where-Q.mk. 'Where(pl)'
20.	(a)	ərowa-me how-Q.mk. 'How'	(b)	ərowa-ərowa-me how-how-Q.mk. 'How(pl)'

They occur in the sentence level.

Examples:-

21. (a) ətu-ətu iskul t^{h}iŋ-ŋe
who-who school go-Q.mk.
'Who(pl) are go to school?'

(b) əmo-nə ì-ì bək-me
he-nom. what-what eat-Q.mk.
'What(pl) is he eat?'

(c) nəŋ hoyke-hoyke t^{h}iŋ-me
you where-where go-Q.mk.
'Where(pl) are you going?'

(d) nəŋ ərowa-ərowa əm-me
you how-how live-Q.mk.
'How(pl) do you live?'

(e) iro-iropə di-me
which-which like-Q.mk.
'Which(pl) do (you) want?'

III. ADVERBS

Examples:-

22.	(a)	sum-mə slow-adv.mk. 'slowly'	(b)	sum-mə-sum-mə slow-adv.mk.-slow-adv.mk. 'slowly and slowly'
23.	(a)	təm-mə much-adv.mk. 'much'	(b)	təm-mə-təm-mə much-adv.mk.-much-adv.mk. 'much and much'
24.	(a)	le-yə again-adv.mk. 'again'	(b)	le-yə-le-yə again-adv.mk.-again-adv.mk. 'again and again'

They occur in the sentences.

Examples:-

25. (a)	nəŋ	bu	summə	summə	bək-ke
	you	cook rice	slowly	slowly	eat-SP
	'You eat rice slowly and slowly.'				
(b)	əmo	tuy	təmmə	təmmə	in-ne
	he	water	much	much	drink-SP
	'He drinks water much and much.'				

IV. VERBS

"In the case of verbs, it differs from other reduplication of nouns, adverbs, adjectives and wh-question words. Reduplication of verb (in certain context) becomes a sentence, and named as sentential reduplication. This is grammatically possible in different types of sentence construction, such as informative statement, command and request" (Yashawanta,1988). In Chothe, such type of sentence constructions are informative statement, command and request. Reduplication of verbs can be treated as a sentence construction of an informative statement, command and request.

A. INFORMATIVE STATEMENT

In this case, the speaker is informing the addressee, occurring just at the moment of departure.

Examples:-

26. $t^hi\eta$-səw-we — $t^hi\eta$-səw-we
go-PER.asp-SP — go-PER.asp-SP
'I am going.'

B. COMMANDS

It is commonly used to express when the speaker urges the addressee to perform the action.

Examples:-

27. (a) bək-ko — bək-ko
eat-com.mk. — eat-com.mk.
'(You) eat.'

(b) $t^hi\eta$-ŋo — $t^hi\eta$-ŋo
go-com.mk. — go-com.mk.
'(You) go.'

III. REQUEST

In Chothe, reduplication of verb can be used as a request construction when the speaker requests the respected persons.

Examples:-

28. (a) bək-pi-o — bək-pi-o
eat-HON.mk.-com.mk. eat-HON.mk.-com.mk.
'Please eat.'

(b) oŋ-pi-o — oŋ-pi-o
sit-HON.mk.-com.mk. sit-HON.mk.-com.mk.
'Please sit.'

(c) in-pi-o — in-pi-o
drink-HON.mk.-com.mk. drink-HON.mk.-com.mk.
'Please drink.'

NINE

SENTENCE PROCESS

It is the study of sentence-building, of the ways in which words are arranged together in order to make a large unit.

"A traditional term for the study of the rules governing the way words are combined to form sentences in a language. An alternative definition(avoiding the concept of 'word') is the study of the interrelationships between elements of sentence structure, and of the rules governing the arrangement of sentences in sequences," (Crystal, 1985).

According to Robins (1964), "Traditionally the longest structure within which a full grammatical analysis is possible has been taken as the sentence."

Most linguistic definitions of the sentence show the influence of the American linguist Leonard Bloomfield, who pointed to the structural autonomy, or independence, of the notion of sentence:- it is " not included by virtue of any grammatical construction in any larger linguistic form". Recent research has attempted to discover comparable to the sentence, whose constituent structure is stateable in formal, distributional terms. The point of Bloomfield's definition can be stated more concisely as follows:- the sentence is the largest unit of grammatical description.

In Chothe, the normal order of words in sentence is SOV (Subject-Object-Verb). The word order is the same for all the types of basic sentences of declaratives, interrogatives and imperatives.

Sentence process can be divided into four types:- (a) Declarative sentences (b) Negative sentences (negation) (c) Interrogative sentences and (d) Imperative sentences.

DECLARATIVE SENTENCES

Declarative sentences are said to be statements which affirm or danay something. An affirmative of declarative means that the speaker believes the proposition is true. "But it is quite common to use declaratives without believing to proposition to the true," (Hudson, 1975). Declaratives may be used as sentence forms for putting forward a claim, an opinion or a judgement or a proposition the speaker believes to be true. In Chothe, the sufix **e~ye~ke~ŋe~ne~te~wẹ~pe~le,** etc. are suffixed to the verbal roots or stems to form the declarative sentence. The suffixes are treated as a sentence particle(SP). The suffixes **e~we~ye** occur with the vowels and approximant, and others are lengthen the consonants (see simple sentence).

NEGATION

Generally, there are two types of negative formation that appear in many languages. One is formed by verbal modifiers such as **not, never, hardly,** etc., in English and **nai** in Japanese (sentence negation). The other type of negation is formed by negative prefixes such as **in-, dis-, un-, im-** in English and **hi-, hu-, mu-** etc. in Japanese (affixial negation). In Chothe, simple negation is formed by the suffixation of negative marker **-no** to the verbal root. It may or may not be followed by a sentence particle(SP) **-we** after the negative marker **-no**. If the SP occurs, it becomes more formal structure of sentences. [a^{S} are affirmative sentences while b^{S} are negative sentences]

Examples:-

1. (a^{S}) kəy bu bək-ke
   I cook rice eat-SP
   'I eat rice.'

(b^S) kəy bu bək-no-we
I cook rice eat-neg.-SP
'I do not eat rice.'

The negative marker **-no** is also suffixed to the unrealised aspect marker and followed by sentence particle **-we** as in the examples (2b^S).

Examples:-

2. (a^S) kəy iskul tʰiŋ-ŋəŋ-ŋe
I school go-UNR.asp-SP
'I will go to school.'

(b^S) kəy iskul tʰiŋ-ŋəŋ-no-we
I school go-UNR.asp.-neg.-SP
'I will not go to school.'

In Chothe, there are three types of negative markers. They are as follows:-

(i) **-no** is used to negate a positive statement,

(ii) **-ləw/-rəw** is used in morphological level, and

(iii) **ano** is used as a lexicalized negator.

They are discussed one by one in the following.

I. -no

In Chothe, the negative marker **-no** is used to negate a positive statement by adding to the verbal roots or stems. The negative marker **-no** can be used in different negative sentences i.e. (a) simple negative sentences (b) future negative sentences (c) command negative sentences and (d) question negative sentences.

A. SIMPLE NEGATIVE SENTENCES

The negative marker **-no** is added to the verbal roots or stems and is followed by the SP in the simple negation. [a^S are the positive sentences while b^S are negative sentences]

Examples:-

3. (a^S) kəy — əmo — dəŋ-ŋe
   I — he — know-SP
   'I know him.'

   (b^S) kəy — əmo — dəŋ-no-we
   I — he — know-neg.-SP
   'I do not know him.'

4. (a^S) əmo — ju — in-ne
   he — liquor — drink-SP
   'He drinks liquor.'

   (b^S) əmo — ju — in-no-we
   he — liquor — drink-neg.-Sp
   'He does not drink water.'

B. FUTURE NEGATIVE SENTENCES

In this form, the negative marker **-no** is also added to the verbal roots or stems after the unrealised aspect marker **-əŋ~kəŋ ~ŋəŋ~nəŋ~məŋ**, etc. and is followed by the sentence particle(SP).

Examples:-

5. (a^S) əmo — wa-əŋ-ŋe
   he — come-UNR.asp-SP
   'He will come.'

   (b^S) əmo — wa-əŋ-no-we
   he — come-UNR.asp-neg.-SP
   'He will not come.'

6. (a^S) kəy — ju — in-nəŋ-ŋe
   I — liquor — drink-UNR.asp-SP
   'I shall drink liquor.'

   (b^S) kəy — ju — in-nəŋ-no-we
   I — liquor — drink-UNR.asp-neg.-SP
   'I shall not drink liquor.'

C. COMMAND NEGATIVE SENTENCES

There are two types of negation in imperative sentences. They are:- (a) Prohibitive and (b) Let negative.

I. PROHIBITIVE

The negative marker **-no** is added to the verbal roots or stems before the command marker **-o~wo** for making prohibitive.

Examples:-

7.	(a^S)	(nəŋ)	bu	bək-ko
		(you)	cook rice	eat-com.mk.
		'(You) Eat rice.'		

	(b^S)	(nəŋ)	bu	bək-no-wo
		(you)	cook rice	eat-neg.-com.mk.
		'(You) Don't eat.'		

8.	(a^S)	(nəŋ)	t^hiŋ-ŋo
		(you)	go-com.mk.
		'(You) Go.'	

	(b^S)	(nəŋ)	t^hiŋ-no-wo
		(you)	go-neg.-com.mk.
		'(You) Don't go.'	

II. LET NEGATIVE

The negative marker **-no** is directly added to the verbal roots or stems for making "Let" negative and is followed by the proposal marker **"səruy"**.

Examples:-

9.	(a^S)	əni	bu	bək-səruy
		our	cook rice	eat-prop.mk.
		'Let us eat rice.'		

	(b^S)	əni	bu	bək-no-səruy
		our	cook rice	eat-neg.-prop.mk.
		'Let us not eat rice.'		

10. (a^s) əni ju in-səruy
our liquor drink-prop.mk.
'Let us drink liquor.'

(b^s) əni ju in-no-səruy
our liquor drink-neg.-prop.mk.
'Let us not drink liquor.'

D. QUESTION NEGATIVE SENTENCES

There are two interrogative markers in Chothe. They are **-mo** and **-me**. The interrogative marker **-mo** is the yes/no question marker and the interrogative marker **-me** is the wh-question marker. In the formation of negative question, the negative marker **-no** is directly added to the verbal roots or stems, then it is followed by the question marker **-me** or **-mo**.

Examples:-

11. (a^s) ətu-nə əmo-tə liŋləy-me
who-nom. he-acc. love-Q.mk.
'Who loves him?'

(b^s) ətu-nə əmo-tə liŋləŋ-no-me
who-nom. he-acc. love-neg.-Q.mk.
'Who doesn't love him?'

12. (a^s) nəŋ əmo-tə liŋləy-mo
you he-acc. love-Q.mk.
'Do you love him?'

(b^s) nəŋ əmo-tə liŋləy-no-mo
you he-acc. love-neg.-Q.mk.
'Don't you love him?'

II. –ləw/-rəw

The negative marker **–ləw/-rəw** is used in the morphological level.

Examples:-

13. (a^{S})	ə-pəŋ-pə	mi
	F.P.-fool-NZ	man
	'Foolish man'	
(b^{S})	pəŋ-ləw-pə	mi
	fool-neg.-NZ	man
	'Clever man' (neg. + foolish man)	

14. (a^{S})	ə-siŋ-pə	mi
	F.P.-wise-NZ	man
	'Wise man'	
(b^{S})	siŋ-ləw-pə	mi
	wise-neg.-NZ	man
	'Unwise man' (neg. + wise man)	

15. (a^{S})	ə-luŋsa-pə	mi
	F.P.-angry-NZ	man
	'Angry man'	
(b^{S})	luŋsa-ləw-pə	mi
	angry-neg.-NZ	man
	'Gentleman' (neg. + angry man)	

The negative marker **–ləw/-rəw** is suffixed to the non finite verbs which function as adjective modifying the noun in the morphological level.

Examples:-

16. (a^{S})	hi-na-hi	in-nəŋ-pə	ju-ye
	pdet-away-pdet	drink-pot.-NZ	liquor-SP
	'This is the liquor to drink.'		
(b^{S})	hi-na-hi	in-nəŋ-ləw-pə	ju-ye
	pdet-away-pdet	drink-pot.-neg.-NZ	liquor-SP
	'This is the liquor not to drink.		

In the above sentence (16a-b), **in-nəŋ-pə** and **in-nəŋ-ləw-pə** are non finite verbs (particularized) which function as adjective modifying the noun **ju** "liquor".

III. ano (LEXICALIZED NEGATOR)

Various languages of the world, namely Tongan, Fijian Maori (of Loninesian), Diegueno, Majave (of Yunan languages), Evenki (of Siberian group of Tungus family), Nenets, Nganasan (of Samoyedic languages), Erzja (of Mordvin languages), Udmurt, Komi-Zyrian Komi-Permjak (of Permic languages) and dialects of Lappish, Estonian, Livonian, Veps have negative verb or auxiliary verb or as both.

Like these languages, Chothe has negative verb functioning as a higher verb. The lexicalized negator **ano** is a negative verb which occurs in the sentence final position, it gives the information about the simple expression to the familiar persons or juniors. The lexicalized negator **ano** is a negative form of copula verb - **e~ye~we~ke ~ŋe~me ~ne~le**, etc.

Examples:-

17. (a) əmo dimho-e
he Dimho-be
'He is Dimho.'

(b) əmo dimho ano
he Dimho be not
'He is not Dimho.'

18. (a) hi-na-hi uy-ye
pdet-away-pdet dog-be
'This is a dog.'

(b) hi-na-hi uy ano
pdet-away-pdet dog be not
'This is not a dog.'

If the copula verb **-we** is added to the lexicalized negator **ano**, it will be more formal and is used in reporting to the respected persons or seniors.

Examples:-

19. (a) kəy coŋte-ye
I Chongte-be
'I am Chongte.'

(b) kəy coŋte ano-we
I Chongte be not-be
'I am not Chongte.'

"A negative verb always at least some of the properties of regular verbs, such as occurrence with a verbal complementizer, or inflection for mood, tense, aspect, person or number," (Pyne, 1984).

In Chothe, the negator **ano** can be treated as a negative verb on the basis of Pyne's definition. This negator **ano** has one more aspect i.e. progresive aspect.

Example:-

20. kəy iskul t^{h}iŋ-pə ano-hoŋ-ŋe
I school go-NZ be not-prog.-SP
'I am not yet going to school.'

The lexicalized negator **ano** is changed to **ani** before the emphatic suffix **–yəw** as in the example(21) and is followed by the sentence particle.

Example:-

21. əmo in-keyə əm-pə mi ani-yəw-we
he house-loc. live-NZ man be not-emph.-SP
'Now he is not a member of our family.'

The lexicalized negator **ano** can function as a free negative, reply to a question.

Examples:-

22. (a) əmo ət^{h}im-mo
he doctor-Q.mk.
'Is he doctor?'

(b) ano
'No'

DOUBLE NEGATION

In mathematics and algebra, there is a principle or formula that two negatives become a positive. But "Language is not mathematics"(Jespersen, 1924). What can be applied to mathematics can not be applied to language: Jespersen gives here his opinion........................" wherever two negatives really refer to the same idea or word (as special negatives) the result is invariably positive...................... (Jespersen,1924). In Chothe, there are two types of double negation. They are:- (i) **-no** occurs twice, and (ii) **-no** with **ano**.

I -no and -no

The neative marker **-no** occurs twice , to express the action decided to be done.

Examples:-

23. (a) kəy tʰiŋ-no-pə ŋay-no-we
I go-neg.-NZ agree-neg.-SP
'It is not that I should not go.'
(in the sence : you may do anything, but I should go.)

(b) kəy tʰiŋ-no-pə ŋay-no-we
I go-neg.-NZ agree-neg.-SP
'It cannot be agreed that I should not go.'
(because I have something to do there.)

II. -no with ano

In Chothe, double negation is also formed by adding the negative marker **-no** and by occurring lexicalized negator **ano** in a sentence. In this case, the event can occur in any time, that is, in past or present or future. It is used in simple expression with a positive sense.

Examples:-

24.	kəy	bu	bək-no-pə	ano-we
	I	cook rice	eat-neg.-NZ	lex.neg.-SP

'It is not that I don't eat rice.'

25.	kəy	ju	in-nəŋ-no-pə	ano-we
	I	liquor	drink-UNR.asp.-neg.-NZ	lex.neg.-SP

'It is not that I will not drink liquor.'

But in some contexts the two negatives do not exactly become the positive one. For example, "not uncommon" is not identical with "common" of their result. The meaning expressed by "not uncommon" is weaker than that expressed by "common" (Jespersen,1924). Such types of negative formation are found in Chothe.

Examples:-

26. (a)	əmo	t^ha-no-pə	ano-we
	he	good-neg.-NZ	lex.neg.-SP

'He is not not-good.'

(b)	əmo	t^ha-ye
	he	good-SP

The sentence (26b) has stronger meaning than the meaning expressed by the sentence (26a).

NEGATIVE STRENGTHENING AND NEGATIVE POLARITY

Generally, negative is strengthened through some additional words. In French the normal form for negation has been strengthened by the accrual of postverbal elements like **mic** "crump" **point** "a point", especially **pas** "a step". The word selected for this strengthening effect may be an adverbial element, either intrinsically negative (English **not nothing**, German **nict**) or originally positive forms (like Danish **ikka** "not") which acquired a negative signification through constant employment in negative sentence, (Jespersen, 1917).

In Chothe, negation is strengthened by the addition of a prefix **suk-**. The negative strengthening element **suk-** is a negative polarity item and it is prefixed to the verbal roots or stems. It is used in the negative environment only but the verbal root is reduplicated as in sentence (27b).

Examples:-

27. (a) kəy ju in-no-we
I liquor drink-neg.-SP
'I don't take liquor.'

(b) kəy ju suk-in in-no-we
I liquor neg.pol-drink drink-neg.-SP
'I don't take liquor at all.'

28. (a)* kəy ju suk-in-no-we

(b)* kəy ju suk-in in-nəŋ-ŋe

In the above examples, (28a) and (28b) are ungrammartical because in (28a) **suk-** is prefixed to the verb **in** "drink" but the verb **in** "drink" is not reduplicated and the prefix **suk-** is used only in the negative environment, but in (28b) **suk-** occurs in the positive environment.

As discussed earlier, indefinite pronouns:- **ikum** "no one/none" **ətukum~ətukummə** "not anyone", etc. are used in negative environment only (see Indefinite pronoun).

In Chothe, there are some negative question sentences which can express a positive meaning. The speaker uses the negative question to give his opinion, the meaning is positive.

Example:-

29. (a) mənu-nə əsənaw-tə liŋləy-no-mo
mother-nom. son-acc. love-neg.-Q.mk.
'Does not mother love her son?'

In the above sentence (29), the speaker uses the negative question to give his opinion that every mother loves her son, the sentence expresses a positive meaning.

There are also some positive interrogative sentences which can express negative meanings. In this case, semantically, the sentence expresses negative meaning in which the negative element is not present in the surface structure.

Examples:-

30. (a) ilupa-tə | ətu-nə | liŋləy-me
thief-acc. | who-nom. | love-Q.mk.
'Who loves the thief?'

(b) tʰa-rəw-pə | mi-tə | ətu-nə | liŋləy-me
good-neg.-NZ | man-acc. | who-nom. | love-Q.mk.
'Who loves the bad man?'

In the above sentences (30a-b), the speaker expresses his opinion that nobody loves the thief of the bad man, but the sentence does not have the negative marker and also the speaker uses these sentences to ask about the opinion of the addressee. The addressee may reply that nobody loves the thief or the bad man.

In Chothe, the prefixes **i-** and **pəŋ-** are used both in the positive environment as well as negative environment. These prefixes are added to the verbal roots or stems. The verbal root or stem is reduplicated. They are given below:-

I. POSITIVE ENVIRONMENT

It is found without the negative marker **-no**, but the verbal roots or stems are reduplicated.

Examples:-

31. əmo | i-bək | bək-ke
he | almost-eat | eat-SP
'He eats (almost).'

32. əmo | pəŋ-bək | bək-ke
he | almost-eat | eat-SP
'He eats (almost).'

In the above sentences (31) and (32), the prefixes **i-** and **pəŋ-** are added to the verb **bək** "eat", then the verb **bək** "eat" is reduplicated.

II. NEGATIVE ENVIRONMENT

It is formed with the negative marker **-no**. The verbal roots or stems are reduplicated.

Examples:-

33. əmo i-bək bək-no-we
 he almost-eat eat-neg.-SP
 'He doesn't eat (almost).'

34. əmo pəŋ-bək bək-no-we
 he almost-eat eat-neg.-SP
 'He does not eat (almost).'

In the above sentences (33) and (34), the prefixes **i-** and **pəŋ-** are added to the verb **bək** "eat", then the verb **bək** "eat" is reduplicated. The negative marker **-no** is also suffixed to the verb **bək** "eat" to make the environment a negative.

The suffix **–həp** is also used in both the positive and negative environments. The marker **–həp** is suffixed to the verbal roots or stems. The verb is not reduplicated in its suffixation.

Examples:-

35. (a) əmo bək-həp-pe
 he eat-everything(without tasty)-SP
 'He eats everything (without tasty).'

 (b) əmo bək-həp-no-we
 he eat-everything(without tasty)-neg.-SP
 'He does not eat a lot.' (He eats a little.)

INTERROGATIVE SENTENCES

A sentence that asks for information is called an interrogative sentence. "The mood category is associated with question. A few languages have distinctive verbal inflections for this purpose, but the interrogative mood is more commonly expressed by particles, by distinctive word order or merely by intonation", (Trask,1991).

"Most languages discriminate between two types of questions:- (a) special, partial or nexus-questions which may be answered by "yes" or "no" : **Is John building a house?**, and (b) general, total or x-questions which cannot be so answered and which are usually introduced by an interrogative pronoun, adjective or adverb : **What is John building?** The first type may be expressed by intonation alone, with or without accompanying gesture : **John building a house?** This is the normal word-order for nexus-questions in Chinese. The question requires the solution of a doubt or alternative : **John is - is not- building a house?** The answer is **Building a house** or **Not building a house**. Thus the question contains the substance of the answer and is expressed in the exact order of the answer", (Deutsch,1957).

There are four types of questions in Chothe. They are :- (i) Yes-no questions (ii) Wh-questions (iii) Alternative questions and (iv) Tag questions. Yes-no questions and Wh-questions are major type questions. Alternative questions and Tag questions are the minor type questions.

YES-NO QUESTIONS

It is a question which expects one of the answers "yes" or "no". In many languages, a terminal rising contour indicates a yes-no question, with or without interrogative markers such as inversion of subject or object, interrogative particles, etc. Information questions in all languages are marked with interrogative words, while many yes/no questions are with special interrogative particles or affixes". (Ultan,1978)

In Chothe, yes-no questions are formed by adding the question marker **-mo** and **-a~ka~ŋa~ma~la~na**, etc. to the nouns, verbs, numerals, etc. They are discussed below:-

I. -mo

It can be marked that the question marker **-mo** is used by the youth and educated persons generally.

Examples:-

36. (a) coŋte-mo
Chongte-Q.mk.
'(Are you) Chongte?'

(b) nəŋ iskul tʰiŋ-mo
you school go-Q.mk.
'Do you go to school?'

(c) mi rəŋa-mo
man five-Q.mk.
'Is it five man?'

The question marker **-mo** occurs with simple, continuous, perfective and unrealised aspects after the verbal roots.

Examples:-

37. (a) əmo bu bək-mo
he cook rice eat-Q.mk.
'Does he eat rice (meal)?'

(b) əmo bu bək-kəm-mo
he cook rice eat-CON.asp-Q.mk.
'Is he eating rice (meal)?'

(c) əmo bu bək-səw-mo
he cook rice eat-PER.asp-Q.mk.
'Has he taken rice (meal)?'

(d) əmo bu bək-kəŋ-mo
he cook rice eat-UNR.asp-Q.mk.
'Will he eat rice (meal)?'

II. -a~ka~ŋa~ma~la~na, etc.

The question marker **-a~ka~ŋa~ma~la~na,** etc. are used to

informal speeches and are used by the uneducated old people. The question marker **-a** is added to the vowel ending roots or stems. Others occur after the consonant ending and are lengthened.

Examples:-

38. (a) kəydi-a
kaidi-Q.mk.
'(Are you) Kaidi?'

(b) nəŋ tʰiŋ-ŋa
you go-Q.mk.
'Do you go?'

(c) mi intʰum-ma
man three-Q.mk.
'Is it three man?'

Wh-QUESTIONS

In Wh-Questions, the question marker **-me** is added to the Wh-question words and the verbal roots. It also occurs with simple, continuous, perfective and unrealised aspects. The question words may be an interrogative pronoun or an interrogative adverb. The interrogative pronouns are:- **ətu-me** "who", **i-me** "what", **əropə-me** "which", **ətuta-me** "whose", etc. The interrogative adverbs are:- **hoyke-me/ike-me** "where", **ikena-me/hoykena-me** "From where", **ijenə-me/iyenə-me/iyəŋŋə-me** "why", **itikkə-me/iropəkankeyə-me** "when", **ərowa-me/irowa-me** "how", etc. They are as follows:-

ətu-me "who"

ətu is the Wh-question word and **-me** is the question marker. The question marker **-me** can suffix to the Wh-question word **ətu** and the verbal roots. It is also occurred with simple, continuous, perfective and unrealised aspects.

Examples:-

39. (a) nəŋ ətu-me
you who-Q.mk.
'Who are you?'

(b) əmo ətu-nə huk-me
he who-nom. beat-Q.mk.
'Who has he beaten?'

(c) ətu-nə tulu-ha e-əm-me
who-nom. work-ddet do-CON.asp-Q.mk.
'Who is doing the work?'

(d) ətu-nə tulu-ha e-səw-me
who-nom. work-ddet do-PER.asp-Q.mk.
'Who has done the work?'

(e) ətu-nə tulu-ha e-əŋ-me
who-nom. work-ddet do-UNR.asp-Q.mk.
'Who will do the work?'

In the above examples (39c-d), the nominative case suffix –**nə** is added to the Wh-question word **ətu** "who". The other case suffixes **–tə, -ke, -kena** and **-rit** are also added to the Wh-question word **ətu** "who".

Examples:-

40. (a) əmo-nə ətu-tə kok-me
he-nom. who-acc. call-Q.mk.
'Whom does he call?'

(b) əmo-nə əbay-ha ətu-ke pe-me
he-nom. book-ddet who-loc. give-Q.mk.
'To whom has he given the book?'

(c) əmo-nə ətu-kena əbay la-me
he-nom. who-abl. book take-Q.mk.
'From whom does he take the book?'

(d) əmo ətu-rit t^{h}iŋ-me
he who-asso. go-Q.mk.
'With whom does he go?'

ì-me "What"

ì is the Wh-question word and **-me** is the question marker. The question marker **-me** can suffix to the wh-question word **ì** and the verbal roots. It is also occurred with simple, continuous, perfective and unrealised aspects.

Examples:-

41. (a) ì-me
what-Q.mk.
'What (is it)?'

(b) nəŋ ì di-me
you what like-Q.mk.
'What do you want?'

(c) nəŋ ì bək-kəm-me
you what eat-CON.asp-Q.mk.
'What are you eating?'

(d) nəŋ ì bək-səw-me
you what eat-PER.asp-Q.mk.
'What have you eaten?'

(e) nəŋ ì bək-kəŋ-me
you what eat-UNR.asp-Q.mk.
'What will you eat?'

əropə-me "Which"

əropə and **-me** are the wh-question word and question marker respectively. The question marker **-me** occurs with the wh-question word **əropə** and the verbal roots. It also occurs with simple, perfective and unrealised aspects.

Examples:-

42. (a) mi-ha əropə-me
man-ddet which-Q.mk.
'Which is the man?'

(b) nəŋ əropə di-me
you which like-Q.mk.
'Which do you want?'

(c) əmo əropə la-səw-me
he which take-PER.asp-Q.mk.
'Which has he taken?'

(d) nəŋ / əropə / la-əŋ-me
you / which / take-UNR.asp-Q.mk.
'Which will you take?'

The nominative suffix **–nə** occurs with the **əropə** "which" (the wh-question word).

Example:-

43. pun-hi / əropə-nə / ənt^ha-me
cloth-ddet / which-nom. / beauty-Q.mk.
'Which one is beautiful between the clothes?'

ətuta-me "Whose"

ətuta is the question word and **-me** is the question marker. The question marker **-me** can be added to the wh-question word **ətuta** and the nouns.

Examples:-

44. (a) əbay-hi / ətuta-me
book-pdet / whose-Q.mk.
'Whose book is this?'

(b) ətuta / pun-me
whose / cloth-Q.mk.
'Whose cloth (is this)?'

ike-me/hoyke-me "where"

ike/hoyke is the question word and **-me** is the question marker. The question marker **-me** can be added to the wh-question word **ike/hoyke** and the verbal roots.

Examples:-

45. (a) hoy-ke-me
where-loc.-Q.mk.
'Where (are you going)?'

(b) əmo / hoy-ke / t^hiŋ-me
he / where-loc. / go-Q.mk.
'Where does he go?'

ikena-me/hoykena-me "From where"

ikena/hoykena is the wh-question word and **-me** is the question marker. The question marker **-me** can be added to the wh-question word **ikena/hoykena** and the verbal roots.

Examples:-

46. (a) hoy-kena-me
where-from-Q.mk.
'From where (are you going)?'

(b)

əmo	hoy-kena	wa-me
he	where-from	come-Q.mk.

'From where does he come?'

iyenə-me/ijenə-me/iyəŋŋə-me "Why"

iyenə/ijenə/iyəŋŋə is the wh-question word and **-me** is the question marker. The question marker **-me** can be suffixed to the wh-question word **iyenə/ijenə/iyəŋŋə** and the verbal roots.

Examples:-

47. (a)

nəŋ-nə	t^hiŋ-pə-ha	iyəŋŋə-me
you-nom.	go-NZ-ddet.	why-Q.mk.

'Why were you going?'

(b)

nəŋ	iyəŋŋə	t^hiŋ-me
you	why	go-Q.mk.

'Why are you going?'

In the above example, (47a) is used to ask about the information regarding the reason of going but the way of action occurs at a remote situation. The speaker asked the question in the strong emotion. The above example, (47b) is used to ask about the reason but the way of action accurs at present situation in the simple way.

itikkə-me/əropəkankeyə-me "When"

itikkə/əropəkankeyə is the wh-question word and **-me** is the question marker. The question marker **-me** can be added to the wh-question word **itikkə/əropəkankeyə** and the verbal roots.

Examples:-

48. (a) itikkə-me
when-Q.mk.
'When (the time)?'

(b)

nəŋ	itikkə	əbay-ha	pe-me
you	when	book-ddet	give-Q.mk.

'When do you give the book?'

ərowa-me/irowa-me "How"

ərowa/irowa is the wh-question word and **-me** is the question marker. The question marker **-me** can be added to the wh-question word **ərowa/irowa** and the verbal roots.

Examples:-

49. (a) ərowa-me
how-Q.mk.
'How (is it)?'

(b)

əmo-nə	ərowa	se	pe-me
he-nom.	how	money	give-Q.mk.

'How does he give money?'

Repetition of Wh-question (see for detail in Reduplication)

ALTERNATIVE QUESTION

In Chothe, alternative question are formed by adding the question marker **-mo** to both the alternative. The alternatives may be nouns or pronouns or verbs or adverbs. Then, one of the two alternatives can constitute an answer. In the construction of alternative question, **anore** "or" is used as coordinator.

I. ALTERNATIVE OF NOUNS

Examples:-

50. (a)

ə-bək-pə-ha	dimho-mo	anore	coŋte-mo
F.P.-eat-NZ-ddet	Dimho-Q.mk.	or	Chongte-Q.mk.

'Is the eater Dimho or Chongte?'

(b) nəŋ-nə di-pə-ha pun-mo anore liŋlut-mo
you-nom. like-NZ-ddet cloth-Q.mk. or shirt-Q.mk.
'Which cloth or shirt do you like?'

II. ALTERNATIVE OF VERBS

There are two verb phrases in the order of positive verb phrase and negative verb phrase with a coordinate **anore** "or" as a connector of the positive VP and negative VP. The VP is formed with a question marker **-mo** to make an alternative question of verbs.

Examples:-

51. (a) nəŋ bu bək-mo anore bək-no-mo
you rice eat Q.mk. or eat-neg.-Q.mk.
'Do you eat rice or not?'

(b) əmo iskul t^{h}iŋ-ŋəŋ-mo anore t^{h}iŋ-ŋəŋ-no-mo
he school go-UNR.asp-Q.mk. or go-UNR.asp.-neg.-Q.mk.
'Will you go to school or not?'

III. ALTERNATIVE OF ADVERBS

There are two adverb phrases. The two adverb phrases use **anore** "or" as a coordinator of the adverb phrase (Ad.P). The Ad.P is formed with the question marker -mo to make an alternative question of adverbs.

Examples:-

52. (a) əmo-nə wa-pə-ha not-mo anore sum-mo
he-nom. come-NZ-ddet quick-Q.mk. or slow-Q.mk.
'Does he come quickly or slowly?'

(b) nəŋ-nə bu bək-pə-ha təm-mo anore təm-no-mo
you-nom. rice eat-NZ-ddet much-Q.mk. or much-neg.-Q.mk.
'Do you eat rice much or not?'

In the above sentence (52b), the positive Ad.P occurs before the negative Ad.P. Generally, it is used in Chothe.

In the alternative question of nouns, in a sentence, they are coordinated by **anore** "or". It can present two verb phrases. Both the verb phrases may contain positive VP or negative VP.

Examples:-

53. (a) nəŋ əpate-ha huk-kəŋ-mo anore numəyte-ha huk-kəŋ-mo
you boy-ddet beat-UNR. asp-Q.mk. or girl-ddet beat-UNR. asp-Q.mk.
'Will you beat the boy or the girl?'

(b) nəŋ əpate-hahuk-kəŋ-no-mo anore numəyte-ha huk-kəŋ-no-mo
you boy-ddet beat-UNR.asp-neg.-Q.mk. or girl-ddet beat-UNR.asp-neg.-Q.mk.
'Will you not beat the boy or the girl?'

TAG QUESTION

The form of the tag questions should be in agreement with the subject and the verb in the statement. Tag questions are questions attached to sentence on which they are formed. The verbal root of the tag questions are the same as that of the sentence on which the tags are formed. Tag questions are formed with the combination of verbal roots and the question marker **-mo**. The construction of the tag questions are similar to that of the yes-no question. So, a tag question is constructed by the verb-phrase only in Chothe. It may be positive or negative.

I. POSITIVE TAG QUESTION

Example:-

54. əmo iskul tʰiŋ-ŋe, tʰiŋ-mo
he school go-SP go-Q.mk.
'He goes to school, does he?'

Positive tag-question

VP

Verbal root	Aspect	Q.mk.
tʰiŋ	ø	mo
go		Q.mk.

tʰiŋ-mo 'Does(he) go?'

II.NEGATIVE TAG QUESTION

Example:-

55. əmo	iskul	tʰiŋ-ŋe,	tʰiŋ-no-mo
he	school	go-SP	go-neg.-Q.mk.

'He goes to school, doesn't he?'

Negative tag-question

VP

Verbal Root	Aspect	Neg.mk.	Q.mk
tʰiŋ	ø	no	mo
go		neg.	Q.mk.

tʰiŋ-no-mo 'Does not (he) go?'

KIND OF TAG QUESTIONS

In Chothe, tag questions may be reversed tag or constant tag. On the other hand, tag questions can be attached to declarative, imperative and exclamative, both the positive and negative.

REVERSED TAG

As far as the meaning of reversed tag is concerned, the most commonly identified function is "to obtain confirmation" (c.f. Jespersen, 1940; Hudson, 1975). Reversed tag is commonly found in all languages.

It is said to be a reversed tag when the tag question is reversed of that of the proposition. As far as the surface structure is concerned, it will presumably be conceded that the main constituent boundary is in each case marked by a comma, and that each of the major constituents belongs to the category "sentence".

Examples:-

56. (a) əmo ju in-ne, in-no-mo
he liquor drink-SP drink-neg.-Q.mk.
'He drinks liquor, doesn't he?'

(b) əmo ju in-no-we, in-mo
he liquor drink-neg.-SP drink-Q.mk.
'He doesn't drink liquor, does he?'

CONSTANT TAG

Tag question is said to be a constant tag when the tag question is same as that of the proposition. According to Huddleston (1970), "constant polarity tag" has the same polarity as the main sentence. In Chothe, it is used in an ironical or incredulous or deniable sense.

Examples:-

57. (a) əmo ju in-ne, in-mo
he liquor drink-SP drink-Q.mk.
'He drinks liquor, does he?'

(b) əmo ju in-no-we, in-no-mo
he liquor drink-neg.-SP drink-neg.-SP
'He does not drink liquor, doesn't he?'

Both the above two types of examples, (57a-b) are found in Chothe. But the Constant tags are not used frequently.

TAG ON DIFFERENT SENTENCES

In Chothe, tag may be attached to (i) declarative (ii) imperative (iii) interrogative and (iv) exclamative sentences.

I. TAG ON DECLARATIVES

In declarative sentences, positive tag and negative tag questions may be attached. It can be reversed tag or constant tag. There has been a good deal of discussion on tag sentences in transformational grammar (Klima 1964, Katz and Postal 1964, Bolinger 1967, Arbini 1969, Huddleston 1970, Schachter 1973, and Hudson 1975).

A. REVERSED TAG ON DECLARATIVES

Reversed tag may be formed on declarative sentences. "Reversed tag" which is one whose negative-positive polarity in the reverse of that in the main sentence. The most commonly identified function of the reversed polarity tag is to obtain confirmation (Jespersen, 1940) i.e., the speaker thinks the proposition is true, but wants the addressee to confirm it.

Examples:-

58. (a) əmo-nə tulu-ha e-ye, e-no-mo
he-nom. work-ddet do-SP do-neg.-Q.mk.
'He does that work, doesn't he?'

(b) əmo-nə tulu-ha e-no-we, e-mo
he-nom. work-ddet do-neg.-SP do-Q.mk.
'He doesn't do that work, does he?'

In the above examples, (58a-b), the speaker believes that the propositions are true and the reversed tags mean that the speaker wants the addressee to confirm the proposition. In Chothe, tag questions cannot be regarded as optional variant of yes/no questions since they are semantically distinct from yes/no questions.

Examples:-

59. (a) ləy-hi ant^ha-ye ant^ha-no-mo
flower-pdet nice-SP nice-neg.-Q.mk.
'This flower is nice, isn't it?'

(b) əmo-nə coŋte-kena he-yə waŋ-ŋe waŋ-no-mo
he-nom. Chongte-from more-adv.mk. tall-SP tall-neg.-Q.mk.
'He is taller than Chongte, isn't he?'

There are two meanings associated with these propositions. Semantically, one may say that the two reversed tags do emphasize the proposition that "the flower is really nice" in sentence (59a) and that "He is certainly taller than Chongte" in sentence (59b) and make it more precise. A second meaning is one in which it is also possible to say that the two reversed tags is (59a-b) seek confirmation of the propositions from the addressee. The speaker expects only the positive reply from the addressee. The same is the case with the meaning of sentences (59c-d).

Examples:-

59. (c) ləy-hi ənt^{h}a-no-we, ənt^{h}a-mo
flower-pdet nice-neg.-SP nice-Q.mk.
'This flower is not nice, is it?'

(d) əmo-nə coŋte-kena he-yə waŋ-no-we, waŋ-mo
he-nom. Chongte-from more-adv.mk. tall-neg.-SP tall-Q.mk.
'He is not taller than Chongte, is he?'

The most commonly identified function of the reversed tag is to obtain confirmation (Jespersen, 1940) i.e., the speaker thinks the proposition is true, but wants the addressee to confirm it. But it is not necessary for the speaker to be uncertain about the truth of the proposition, as this definition implies (otherwise he wouldn't be asking for confirmation of it). The proposition can be analytically true, in which case the speaker must know for certain is true.

The discussion above leads to the question of the relationship between the meaning of ordinary interrogative and the meaning of a declarative with a tag question. Huddleston (1970) opposes the transformational analysis of Burt (1971) saying that it is surely not true that the interrogative and the declarative with a tag question have the same meaning. Briefly, it can be said that in an interrogative sentence the speaker does not know whether the poposition is true. The speaker simply wants information from the addressee and he does not express his intention on the proposition (he does not take any side of the proposition). But in the declarative with a tag question, the speaker knows whether the proposition is true, and furthermore, he either wants confirmation or wants to give emphasis to the proposition (he expresses his intention). The following examples (60a-c) will support these statements.

Examples:-

60. (a) tʰahoy əntʰa-ye, əntʰa-mo
Thahoi nice-SP nice-Q.mk.
'Thahoi is nice, is she?'

(b) tʰahoy əntʰa-no-ye, əntʰa-no-mo
Thahoi nice-neg.-SP nice-neg.-Q.mk.
'Thahoi is not nice, isn't she?'

(c) tʰahoy əntʰa-mo
Thahoi nice-Q.mk.
'Is Thahoi nice?'

The above examples, (60a-b) are declarative with tag question speaking confirmation or emphasizing the proposition that "Thahoi is or isn't nice." Tags have the function of confirmation (Jespersen, 1940). The function of tag in general seems to be simply that of showing that the speaker is not trying to tell the addressee anything, but rather is expressing shared beliefs (c.f. Cattell, 1973). But, the example (60c) is an ordinary interrogative just looking for information wheather "Thahoi is nice or not", nothing else.

B. CONSTANT TAG ON DECLARATIVES

Constant tag may be formed on declarative sentences. Declaratives are said to be statements which affirm or deny something. "But it is quite common to use declaratives without believing the proposition to be true", (Hudson, 1975). Declaratives may be used as sentence forms for putting forward a claim, an opinion or a judgement or a proposition the speaker believes to be used. Both the negative tag and the positive tag can attach on declarative sentences as a constant tag.

Examples:-

61. (a)

əmo-nə	liŋlut	ək^{h}a	lon-ne,	lon-mo
he-nom	shirt	one	bring-SP	bring-Q.mk.

'He brings a shirt, does he?'

(b)

əmo-nə	liŋlut	ək^{h}a	lon-no-we,	lon-no-mo
he-nom.	shirt	one	bring-neg.-SP	bring-neg.-Q.mk.

'He does not bring a shirt, doesn't he?'

In Chothe, the above two types of constant tags, examples (61a-b) are used in an ironical sense, as denying the truth of the proposition, as an aggressive challenging remark and as incredulous sense, etc. Such types of constant tags are not used frequently.

C. TAG QUESTION WORD anomo

There is a tag question word (T-word) in Chothe, i.e., **anomo** which is used commonly in discourse. Semantically, it is used "to obtain confirmation" and "to express shared beliefs". Syntactically, it is used in both propositions (negative as well as positive) as in sentence (62a-b).

Examples:-

62. (a)

əmo-nə	li-pə-hi	t^{h}əy-ke	nuŋay-ye,	ano-mo
he-nom.	speak-NZ-pdet	hear-loc.	happy-SP	be neg.-Q.mk.

'It is interesting to listen to him, isn't it?'

(b)

əmo-nə	li-pə-hi	t^{h}əy-ke	nuŋay-no-we,	ano-mo
he-nom.	speak-NZ-pdet	hear-loc.	happy-neg.-SP	be neg.-Q.mk.

'It is not interesting to listen to him, isn't it?'

(c)	nəŋ	ju	in-no-we,	ano-mo/in-no-mo
	you	liquor	drink-neg.-SP	be neg.-Q.mk./ drink-neg.-Q.mk.

'You don't take wine, don't you?'

That either the tag **anomo** or **innomo** can be used as seen in the sentence (62c).

The T-word may be used with any declarative.

Examples:-

63. (a)	uni-hi	day-ye,	ano-mo/day-no-mo
	today-pdet	cold-SP	be neg.-Q.mk./cold-neg.-Q.mk.

'Today is cold, isn't it?'

(b)	əmo	waŋ-ŋe,	ano-mo/waŋ-no-mo
	he	tall-SP	be neg.-Q.mk./tall-neg.-Q.mk.

'He is tall, isn't he?'

The T-word is also used in equative sentences

Examples:-

64. (a)	əmo	coŋte-ye,	ano-mo
	he	Çhongte-SP	be neg.-Q.mk.

'He is Chongte, isn't he?'

(b)	əmo	oja	ano-we,	ano-mo
	he	teacher	be neg.-SP	be neg.-Q.mk.

'He is not a teacher, isn't he?'

II. TAG ON IMPERATIVES

Tag questions may be attached to imperative sentences also. It may be divided into three categories:- (a) tag on "you" imperatives (b) tag on "let me" imperatives and (c) tag on "us/him/them" imperatives.

A.I. REVERSED TAG ON "YOU" IMPERATIVES

As for the syntactic constructions of tag question on "you" imperatives where "you" is the underlying. In this case, the speaker wants the proposition to be true. And, the speaker knows that the truth of the proposition clearly depends on whether the addressee wants to make them true. It shows that the addressee complies or not.

Examples:-

65. (a) tulu-ha e-wo, e-əŋ-no-mo
work-ddet do-com.mk. do-UNR.asp-neg.-Q.mk.
'(You,Sg.) Do that work, won't you?'

(b) lu-suy-ke lak^{h}a-no-mo, lak^{h}a-əŋ-mo
rain-fall-loc. play-neg.-com.mk play-UNR.asp-Q.mk.
'Don't play in the rain, will you?'

(c) əhut in-no-wo, in-nəŋ-mo
cigarette drink-neg.-com.mk. drink-UNR.asp-Q.mk.
'Don't smoke, will you?'

The above sentences (65b-c) are also used in the pohibition. It has a deeper connotation which is not overtly apparent in the surface structure. An extra linguistic fact is involved here, that is, a physical threat (beating of the addressee) has preceded the sentences. In this situation, the speaker (the mother) ask the addressee (her son) again and again to stop playing, i.e. in the sentence (65b). Still the child doesn't stop playing. At last she beats the child then says this sentence (65b). The same is the case with the remaining sentence (65c).

A.II. CONSTANT TAG ON "YOU" IMPERATIVES

In this syntactic construction of tag question on "you" is the underlying.The speaker wants the proposition to be true from the addressee. Generally, it is used to the intimate and junior persons.

Examples:-

66. (a) bu bək-ko, bək-kəŋ-mo
cook rice eat-Q.mk. eat-UNR.asp-Q.mk.
'(You,Sg.) Eat rice, will you?'

(b) bu bək-no-wo bək-kəŋ-no-mo
çook rice eat-neg.-Q.mk. eat-UNR.asp.-neg.Q.mk.
'(You,Sg.) Don't eat rice, won't you?'

In the constant tag, the action (of beating) the addressee (the child) precedes the sentence. The mother has already asked the child again and again not to play in rain. But the child still continues. Then the mother beats the child and says the sentence (67a) **lak^{h}a-o** "play (go on)" ironically instead of saying **lak^{h}a-no-wo** "don't play". Regarding sentence (67b), the mother asks the child not to eat because the curry is hot (spicy). But when the child starts eating, he then starts crying because it is spicy. Then, the mother says "eat" and "go on". Here the action is not involved because it is resultative.

Examples:-

67. (a) lak^{h}a-o, lak^{h}a-əŋ-mo
play-com.mk. play-UNR.asp-Q.mk.
'Play (go on), will you?'

(b) bək-ko, bək-kəŋ-mo
eat-com.mk. eat-UNR.asp-Q.mk.
'Eat (go on), will you?'

B.I. REVERSED TAG ON "LET ME" IMPERATIVES

In Chothe, reversed tag on "let me" is used as a request form. It may be used when the proposition is positive. The tag implies that the speaker believes that the addressee knows at least whether the proposition is true or not. In this context, the speaker wants the confirmation from the addressee.

Examples:-

68. kəy-tə bu bək-pi-o, bək-pi-əŋ-no-mo
I.-acc. cook-rice eat-HON.mk.-com.mk. eat-HON.mk.-UNR.asp-neg-Q.mk.
'Let me eat rice, shan't I?'

69.	kəy-tə	ju	in-pi-o,	in-pi-əŋ-no-mo
	I-acc.	liquor	drink-HON.	drink-HON.mk.-
			mk.-com.mk.	UNR.asp-neg.-Q.mk.

'Let me drink liquor, shan't I?'

The above examples, (68) and (69) will be something like this:- It is requested that I shall be kindly allowed to eat rice and it is requested that I shall be kindly allowed to drink liquor respectively.

B.II. CONSTANT TAG ON "LET ME" IMPERATIVES

Constant tag on "Let me" imperatives is also used as request form (It may be positive tag when the proposition is positive). The tag implies that the speaker knows the truth of the proposition. In this context, the speaker wants the confirmation from the addressee.

Examples:-

70. (a)	kəy-tə	bu	bək-pi-o,	bək-pi-əŋ-mo
	I-acc.	cook	eat-HON.mk.	eat-HON.mk.-
		rice	-com.mk.	UNR.asp-Q.mk.

'Let me eat rice, shall I?'

(b)	kəy-tə	ju	in-pi-o,	in-pi-əŋ-mo
	I-acc.	liquor	drink-HON.mk.-	drink-HON.mk.-
			com.mk.	UNR.asp-Q.mk.

'Let me drink liquor, shall I?'

C.I. REVERSED TAG ON "LET US/HIM/THEM" IMPERATIVES

It is used as suggestion, where the apeaker wants the proposition to be true. Then, the tag shows that the speaker wants the addressee to confirm the situation.

Examples:-

71.	kə-ni	bu	bək-səruy,	bək-no-səruy-mo
	PP-pl	rice	eat-sugg.	eat-neg.-sugg-Q.mk.

'Let us eat rice, shan't we?'

72. kə-ni bu bək-no-səruy, bək-səruy-mo
PP-pl rice eat-neg.-sugg eat-sugg-Q.mk.
'Let us not eat rice, shall we?'

The above examples, (71) and (72) show that "it is suggested that we shall eat rice and it is suggested that we shall not eat rice" respectively.

Examples:-

73. əmo-tə bu bək-səruy, bək-no-səruy-mo
he-acc. rice eat-sugg eat-neg.-sugg-Q.mk.
'Let him eat rice, won't he?'

74. əmo-tə bu bək-no-səruy, bək-səruy-mo
he-acc. rice eat-neg.-sugg eat-sugg-Q.mk.
'Let him not eat rice, will he?'

In the above examples, (73) and (74), the propositions are "let" imperatives. The speaker suggests that "he will be allowed to eat and he will not be allowed to eat" respectively.

C.II. CONSTANT TAG ON "LET US/HIM/THEM" IMPERATIVES

In Chothe, constant tag on "let us/him/them" imperatives is used as suggested form of the speaker. It may be positive or negative according to the speaker. In this context, the speaker wants the addressee to confirm the proposition.

Examples:-

75. (a) kə-ni ju in-səruy, in-səruy-mo
pp-pl liquor drink-sugg. drink-sugg.-Q.mk.
'Let us drink liquor, shall we?'

(b) kə-ni ju in-no-səruy, in-no-səruy-mo
PP-pl liwuor drink-neg.-sugg drink-neg-sugg-Q.mk
'Let us not drink liquor, shan't we?'

76. (a)

əmo-tə	ju	in-səruy,	in-səruy-mo
he-acc.	liquor	drink-sugg	drink-sugg-Q.mk.

'Let him drink liquor, will he?'

(b)

əmo-tə	ju	in-no-səruy,	in-no-səruy-mo
he-acc.	liquor	drink-neg.-sugg	drink-neg.-sugg-Q.mk.

'Let him not drink liquor, won't he?'

III. **TAG ON INTERROGATIVES**

When the tag occurs with an interrogative sentence, the tag is in non-interrogative structure. It may be reversed or constant tag.

Examples:-

77. (a)

nəŋ	əmo-tə	li-mo	li-ye/li-no-we
you	he-acc.	see-Q.mk.	see-SP/see-neg.-SP

'Did you see him, yes/no?'

(b)

nəŋ	əmo-tə	huk-pə	ne-əŋ-no-mo,	ne-əŋ-ŋe/ne-əŋ-no-w
you	he-acc.	beat-NZ	can-UNR.asp-neg.-Q.mk	can-UNR.asp-SP/can- UNR.asp-neg-SP

'Can't you beat him, yes/no?'

In the above examples, (77a-b), both the positive and negative tag have occurred simultaneously. As far as meaning is concerned, it is just like yes/no question. The speaker wants only a yes/no answer, not further information. Furthermore, the speaker has no other intentions of making the addressee believe whether the proposition is true or false. It is also found that there is basically no difference in meaning between ordinary yes/no questions and interrogatives with tags as in the above sentence (77a-b). But when the tag is in the imperative, the intention of the speaker is overtly expressed as given in the examples (78a-b).

Examples:-

78. (a)

nə-ŋəy	tutiŋ	kə-ni-ke	wa-əŋ-mo,	wa-wo-de
pp-pl	tom-orrow	pp-pl-loc.	come-UNR.asp-Q.mk.	come-com.mk.-aff.

'Will you come to my residence tomorrow, come (affectionately).'

(b) nəŋ tutiŋ əbay-ha lon-wa-əŋ-mo, lon-wa-wo-de
you tom-orrow book-ddet. bring-come-UNR.asp-Q. bring-come-mk.com.mk.-aff.

'Will you bring the book tomorrow, bring it (affectionately).'

The intention of the speaker is that he wants the addressee to come without fail and close relationship between the speaker and the addressee is also shown by the morpheme **de.**

IV. TAG ON EXCLAMATIVES

If the tag is attached to the exclamative sentences, it can always be taken as reduced "exclamations".

Examples:-

79. (a) iya ənt^{h}a-pə ləy-me ənt^{h}a-mo
how much nice-NZ flower-Q.mk. nice-Q.mk.
'How nice the flower is, is it?'

(b) iya ənt^{h}a-pə numəyte-me, ənt^{h}a-mo
how much nice-NZ girl-Q.mk nice-Q.mk.
'How nice the girl is, is it?'

The above example (79a), the tag **ənt^{h}a-mo** can be given the same analysis as the full interrogative in (79c).

(c) ləy-hi ənt^{h}a-mo
flower-pdet nice-Q.mk.
'Is this flower nice?'

The exclamation like (79a) differs in meaning from interrogative one like (79c), due to the fact that the latter is a question and therefore credits the addressee with as reliable a view as the speaker. Saying (79c) implies that the addressee will agree, but saying (79a) without tag doesn't imply this. In this context, the exclamations (79a-b), the speaker expresses his sudden feeling or emotion. The tag questions are used as a very aggressive challanging remark or as a metaphorical extension where the speaker is pretending to believe the proposition.

IMPERATIVE SENTENCES

The mood category associated with the uttering of commands, as in "Wash your hand". Many languages have no specific grammatical form for this purpose, often employing (like English) the simplest possible form of the verb, but many others have a specialized imperative inflection of the verb, such as Spanish: **ven, venid, venga** and **vengan** are all specialized imperative forms of the verb **venir** "come" (Trask, 1993).

According to Zandvoort (1972) "Imperative sentences the verb takes the imperative affix to denote request, command and permission". On the other hand, Jespersen observed that " the imperative always refers to the future often immediate future".

As imperative sentence is spoken to a person or persons before the speaker. So, its subject is always "you" (the second person) which is omitted.

DIFFERENT TYPES OF IMPERATIVES

In Chothe, the different types of imperatives are constructed through the suffixation of command markers to the verbal roots or stems which are generally regarded as imperative sentences. They are:- (a) Command Imperatives, (b) Prohibitive Command, (c) "Let" Command, (d) Request for polite expression, (e) "Wish" Imperatives, (f) Remote Imperatives, (g) Permission Imperatives, (h) Condition Imperatives and (i) Peremptory Imperatives.

COMMAND IMPERATIVES

Command is formed by adding the command markers to the verbal roots or stems. The command markers are - **o~yo~wò~ko~ŋo ~lo,** etc. The command marker **-o~wo** occurs after the vowels and approximant /w/ and others occur after the consonant which are lengthened.

Examples:-

80. (a) (nəŋ) t^hiŋ-ŋo
(you,Sg.) go-com.mk.
'(You,Sg.) Go.'

(b) (nəŋ) bu bək-ko
(you,Sg.) cook rice eat-com.mk.
'(You,Sg.) Eat rice.'

(c) (nəŋ) hi-na-hi wa-o
(you,Sg.) pdet-away-pdet come-com.mk.
'(You,Sg) Come here.'

PROHIBITIVE COMMAND

In chothe, prohibitive command is also formed through the suffixation of negative marker **-no** to the verbal roots or stems, then it is followed by command marker **-wo.**

Examples:-

81. (a) nəŋ t^hiŋ-no-wo
(you,Sg) go-neg.-com.mk.
'(You,Sg) Don't go.'

(b) (nəŋ) bu bək-no-wo
(you,Sg.) cook rice eat-neg.-com.mk.
'(You.Sg.)Don't eat rice.'

"LET" COMMAND

It is an indirect coomand. "Let" imperative is used with first person or third person subjects. In Chothe, there are three types of "Let" imperatives. They are:- **-pi-o**, **-su-o** and **–səruy**. They are suffixed to the verbal roots or stems to indicate "Let" imperatives.

I. "LET" WITH A FIRST PERSON SINGULAR POSITIVE

The "let" imperative suffix **-pi-o** is used in the first person singular to express the desire of doing an action and taking the addressee's permission for doing the action.

Examples:-

82. (a) kəy-tə in-pi-o
I-acc. drink-HON.mk.-com.mk.
'Let me drink'

(b) kəy-tə bək-pi-o
I-acc. eat-HON.mk.-com.mk.
'Let me eat.'

II. "LET" WITH A FIRST PERSON SINGULAR NEGATIVE

It is formed with a negative marker **-no** which is added just before the honorific marker **-pi** with a command marker **-o~wo**.

Examples:-

83. (a) kəy t^{h}iŋ-no-pi-o
I go-neg.-HON.mk.-com.mk.
'Let me not go.'

(b) kəy bək-no-pi-o
I eat-neg.-HON.mk.-com.mk.
'Let me not eat.'

III. "LET" WITH A FIRST PERSON PLURAL POSITIVE

In this case, "Let" imperative gives the meaning of suggestion both to the hearer and speaker. It is formed by adding **-səruy** after the verbal roots or stems.

Examples:-

84. (a) kə-ni oŋ-səruy
pp-pl sit-sugg.
'Let us sit.'

(b) kə-ni t^{h}iŋ-səruy
pp-pl go-sugg.
'Let us go.'

IV. "LET" WITH A FIRST PERSON PLURAL NEGATIVE

It is formed with the negative marker **-no** which is suffixed to the verbal roots or stems just before the suggestive marker **–səruy.**

Examples:-

85. (a) kə -ni oŋ -no-səruy
pp-pl sit-neg.-sugg.
'Let us not sit.'

(b) kə-ni t^{h}iŋ -no-səruy
pp-pl go-neg.-sugg.
'Let us not go.'

V. "LET" WITH A THIRD PERSON (SINGULAR/ PLURAL) POSITIVE

It is used to indicate an indirect permission in the case of the third person singular and plural. This type of imperative is formed by adding **-su-o** to the verbal roots or stems.

Examples:-

86. (a) əmo wa-su-o
he come-wish-com.mk.
'Let him come.'

(b) mə-ŋəy wa-su-o
PP-pl come-wish-com.mk.
'Let them come.'

VI. "LET" WITH A THIRD PERSON (SINGULAR/ PLURAL) NEGATIVE

In Chothe, the negative marker -no is suffixed to the verbal roots or stems and it is followed by the **-su** "wish" and **-o** "command marker" to indicate the "Let" imperative negative in the case of the third person singular and plural.

Examples:-

87. (a) əmo wa-no-su-o
he come-neg.-wish-com.mk.
'Let him not come.'

(b) mə-ŋəy wa-no-su-o
PP-pl come-neg.-wish-com.mk.
'Let them not come.'

REQUEST FOR POSITE EXPRESSION

In Chothe, request is also constructed through the suffixation of **-pi-o** to the verbal roots or stems. The subject is always "you" which is omitted in the surface structure.

Examples:-

88. (a) ha-na-keyə tʰiŋ-pi-o
ddet-away-loc. go-HON.mk.-com.mk.
'Please go there.'

(b) hi-na-keyə wa-pi-o
pdet-away-loc. come-HON.mk.-com.mk.
'Please come here.'

"WISH" IMPERATIVES

"Wish" imperatives are constructed through the suffixation of -pi-su-o to the verbal roots or stems. Generally, such types of sentences are used for those having third person subjects.

Examples:-

89. (a) əpuləyhu-nə əmo-tə liŋləy-pi-su-o
god-nom. he-acc. love-HON.mk.-wish-com.mk.
'May god love him.'

(b) əpuləyhu-nə mə-ŋəy-tə luŋsi-pi-su-o
god-nom. pp-pl-acc. bless-HON.mk.-wish-com.mk.
'May god bless them.'

REMOTE IMPERATIVES

In Chothe, the action of remote imperative is to perform an action at a distance place (away from the speaker). It is formed by adding **tʰiŋ** "go" and **–yəw** "emphasis" with a command marker **-wo** by adding to the verbal roots or stems.

Examples:-

90. (a) nəŋ ən-tʰiŋ-yəw-wo
you look-go-emph.-com.mk.
'You go and look.'

(b)	nəŋ	bək-tʰiŋ-yəw-wo
	you	eat-go-emph.-com.mk.

'You go and eat.'

PERMISSION IMPERATIVES

It is formed by adding the command marker -**o~yo~wo~ ko~lo,** etc. to the verbal roots or stems.

Examples:-

91. (a)	nəŋ-nə	di-pə	məkʰəy	la-o
	you-nom.	like-NZ	all	take-com.mk

'Take whatever you like.'

(b)	nəŋ-nə	di-pə	məkʰəy	ləy-yo
	you-nom.	like-NZ	all	buy-com.mk.

'Buy whatever you like.'

CONDITION IMPERATIVES

Condition imperatives are constructed through the suffixation of the command marker **-o~yo~wo~ko~ŋo~lo**, etc. to the verbal roots or stems. It has two independent clauses with a connector **anorecu** "otherwise".

Examples:-

92. (a)	(nəŋ)	tʰiŋ-ŋo	anorecu	kəy-nə	nəŋ	huk-kəŋ-ŋe
	(you)	go-com.mk.	othe-rwise	I-nom	you	beat-UNR. asp.-SP

'Go, otherwise I will beat you.'

(b)	(nəŋ)	wa-o	anorecu	kəy-nə	paysa	pe-əŋ-no-we
	(you)	come-com.mk	other-wise	I-nom	money	give-UNR. asp neg.-SP

'Come, otherwise I will not give money.'

PEREMPTORY DECLARATIVES

In Chothe, peremptory declaratives are also expressed as command. They consist of a verb, an unrealised aspect marker with a peremptory marker **-poy** and a sentence particle **-ye**.

Examples:-

93. (a) nəŋ bu ənottə bək-kəŋ-poy-ye
you rice quickly eat-UNR.asp-perem.-SP
'You should eat rice quickly.'

(b) nəŋ iskul ənottə t^hiŋ-ŋəŋ-poy-ye
you school quickly go-UNR.asp-perem.-SP
'You should go to school quickly.'

IMPERATIVES AND OTHER SENTENCES

In Chothe, an imperative sentence can occur with other sentences. They are:- (i) Declaratives and imperatives (ii) Repetition of imperatives (iii) Multiple imperatives and (iv) Interrogatives and imperatives. They are discussed in the following:-

I. DECLARATIVES AND IMPERATIVES

A declarative sentence can occur with an imperative sentence. The boundary of the declarative sentence is marked by a comma.

Examples:-

94. (a) kə-ni bu bək-susəw-we, nəŋ-kum bək-ko
pp-pl rice eat-PER.asp-SP you-also eat-com.mk.
'We have taken rice, you also eat.'

(b) kə-ni bu bək-no-we, nəŋ-kum bək-no-wo
pp-pl rice eat-neg.-SP you-also eat-neg.-com.mk.
'We do not eat rice, you also don't eat.'

II. REPETITION OF IMPERATIVES

In Chothe, repetition of imperatives are also used. The imperative markers are suffixed to the verbal roots or stems.

Examples:-

95. (a) bək-ko bək-ko
eat-com.mk. eat-com.mk.
'(You) Eat.'

(b) oŋ-ŋo oŋ-ŋo
sit-com.mk. sit-com.mk.
'(You) Sit.'

The above examples, (95a-b), "Repetition of verb (in certain context) becomes a sentence, and named as sentential reduplication. Generally reduplication has the meaning of distributiveness, plurality and emphatics", (Yashawanta, 1988). Reduplication of Chothe indicates these meanings.

III. MULTIPLE IMPERATIVES

It is formed with the co-ordinator **hatəyəwkʰəy** "and then" between the two imperative sentences. In this case, the speaker uses such type of multiple imperatives to juniors.

Examples:-

96. (a) nəŋ hinahi wa-o hatəyəwkʰəy tulu-hi e-o
you here come-com.mk and then work-pdet do-com.mk
'You come here and then do this work.'

(b) nəŋ tʰiŋ-ŋo hatəyəwkʰəy əbay-ha lon-wa-o
you go-com.mk and then book-ddet bring-come-com.mk.
'You go and then bring the book.'

Multiple imperatives also occur with the coordinator **anore** "or" and **əkʰakum** "and" (see connectives).

IV. INTERROGATIVES AND IMPERATIVES

An interrogative sentence can occur with an imperative sentence. The boundary of the interrogative sentence is a comma. It is used when the speaker expects something from the addressee.

Examples:-

97. (a) nəŋ əsaŋ tʰiŋ-ŋəŋ-mo, kə-ta kekok əkʰa juy-wa-o
you Imphal go-UNR.asp-Q.mk. pp-gen. shoe one buy-come-com.mk.
'Will you go to Imphal, buy a shoe for me?'

(b) nəŋ əpʰəy tʰiŋ-ŋəŋ-mo, kə-ta liŋlut əkʰa juy-wa-o
you market go-UNR.asp- pp-gen. shirt one buy-come
Q.mk. -com.mk

'Will you go to market, buy a shirt for me?'

TEN

SOCIAL GRAMMAR

TABOO

Taboo is a Polynesian word denoting "sacred", consecrated on the one hand and uncanny, dangerous forbidden, unclear on the other. The converse of taboo in Polynesian is "noa" which means "common" or generally accessible (Frued, 1950). If a word is struck by a taboo bar, it must be replaced by a harmless alternative, so called "noa" term. Such customs are by no means confined to primitive or less civilized societies, they occur in all kinds of environments and at every level of civilization (Adler, 1978). Frued (1950) also reports that they were current amongst the ancient Romans, Greeks and Hebrews, whose terms were the same as Polynesian taboo. They occur with anologous terms in many other races in America, Africa (Madagascar) and North and Central Asia.

"Taboo is one way in which a society expresses its disapproval of certain kinds of behaviour believed to be harmful to its members, either for supernatural reasons or because such behaviour is held to violate a moral code. Consequently, so far as language is concerned, certain things are not to be said or certain objects can be referred to only in certain circumstances, for example, only by certain people, or through deliberate circumlocutions, i.e. euphemistically. Of course, there are always those who are prepared to break the taboos in an attempt to show their own freedom from such restrictions or to expose the taboos as irrational and unjustified, as in certain movements for "free speach", (Wardhaugh, 1986).

Wundt(1906) describes taboo as the oldest human unwritten code of laws. In some cases it has an intelligible meaning but in some cases it is quite incomprehensible, taboo of latter types are concerned with trivial details and seem to be purely ceremonial in nature.

Haas (1951) has pointed out that certain language taboos seem to arise from bilingual situations. She cites the examples of the Greeks of Oklahoma, whose avoidance of the Greek words **fakki** "soil", **apiswa** "meat", and **apissi** "fat" increased as they used more and more English. A similar avoidance can sometimes be noticed among Thai students learning English in English-speaking countries. They avoid Thai words like **fag** "sheath" and **phrig** "(chilli) pepper" in the presence of anglophones of the phonetic resemblance of these words to certain taboo English words. Thai speakers also often find it difficult to say the English words **yet** and **key** because their sound very much like the Thai words **jed**, a vulgar word for "to have intercourse", and **khii** "excrement". In certain circumstances, personal names may even be changed as a speaker of one language finds that his or her name causes embarrassment in a different linguistic framework, e.g., the Vietnamese name **phuc** in an analophone group.

Certain words are not allowed to be uttered under certain circumstances, at certain places and the like. "In many speech communities certain improper speech forms are uttered only under restricted circumstances; a speaker who utters them outside the restriction is shamed or punished. The strictness of prohibition ranges from a mild rule of propriety to a severe taboo" (Bloomfield, 1933). In place of such forbidden words, it is necessary to use some kind of figurative paraphrases, euphemisms circumlocutions and other linguistic levies, so as to render the speech more polite and acceptable.

In Chothe, uttering the name of a dead person is prohibited under normal circumstances. When circumstances compel them to refer to the deceased person they have to use some circumlocution such as **əmnot^{h}iŋpa** " the person (male) who is no more alive" and **əmnotʰiŋnu** "the person (woman) who is no more alive". The kin terms, that is, **kəpə** "my father", **kənu** "my mother", **kəpu** "my grandfather", **kəpi** "my grandmother", **kəjupa/kəpisəy** "my husband" **kəjunu/kənuməy** "my wife", **kəsinawpa** "my son", **kəsinawnu** "my daughter", etc. are used with the **əmnotʰiŋpa** for man and **əmnotʰiŋnu** for woman.

The prohibition against uttering the name of the dead person is extremely widespread. It is expressed in a variety of ways and has had important consequences. It is found amongst the Australians and Polynesians, the Samoyedh of Siberia, the Todas of Southern India, the Mongols of Tartary, the Tuarego of the Sahara, the Ainos of Japan, the Akamba and Nandi of Central Africa, the Tinguians of the Philippines and the inhabitants of the Nicobar Islands, of Bornea, of Madagascar and of Tasmania (Frazer, 1911b).

In general, husband and wife do not address one another by their respective names. However, husbands are permitted to use the names of their wives but it is considered to be a sin for a wife even to pronounce the name of her husband. A husband is always stated to be superior to his wife. A wife does not pronounce her husband's name but call him by some ejaculations or tecknonyms. This holds true among the Muslim of India, who are mostly coverts from Hinduism (Masani, 1966). Normally, a wife will not utter the name of her husband, her father-in-law, mother-in-law, grandmother-in-law, grandfather-in-law, elder brothers, elder sisters, etc. although this restriction may sometimes be expanded to include all of a wife's elder affines.

A wife uses some displaced words instead of the husband's name. For example, a wife generally calls **tʰəymo** "do you hear?" or **məpa** "his father" to her husband in the sense of attention without using any address term.

It is also forbidden to address people who are older than the speaker by their personal names. It shows that seniority is a complement in Chothe society. It is a kind of social restriction imposed on people so as to maintain harmony in the society. If there was a conflict, the older ones had the authority to settle the disputes. If a person addresses his elder's name, the person would be considered to be highly impolite and ill-mannered.

During the monarchical rule it was taboo to use the names of kings as personal names by their subjects. They use the word **reŋpa** "king" and **reŋnu** "queen" as personal names. It is taboo to use the name of ancestral deity, that is, **pakʰəŋpa** and **soraren**. They use in the respect form of address **pu. pakʰəŋpa** and **pu.soraren.** In the personal names, they use **pu** as the respect form of address for man and **pi** as the respect form of address for woman.

The names of dangerous animals namely **əkəy** "tiger" and **əruy** "snake" are not allowed to be uttered particularly at forest. In place of these animals, Chothe use the word **ləmmuypu** "king of land" for tiger and **tʰiŋna** "grass" for snake . Similar use of euphemisms for dangerous animals like "tiger" is also found in Maharashtrian as **mama** "maternal uncle" in Annam as "grand-father" or "lord". A euphemistic word for "snake" is also found in Kanara, where the word used is "insect or worm", Marathas call it "the long thing" or merely "animal" and Sindhi Muslims call it "rope" (Masani, 1966). It is belived that if the euphemistic term for tiger is used, then the speaker would be left untouched by the tiger and if the euphemistic term for snake is used, it spoils the power of poison. When people go hunting, they do not utter the name of the animal to be hunted. They use the general term **əsa** "animal". This may be compared to "hunters taboo" (Emeneau, 1948).

In Chothe, **hoy** "yes" is a taboo at night. It is belived that the ghosts call the person whenever they want human beings, they will call the particular person by name. If the person happens to answer **hoy** "yes" the ghost or spirit will have its control over them and they belive will die soon. So, they use circumlocution words, that is, **ime** "what" and **ətume** "who". These words can dispel the spirit or ghost, so nothing will happen to the person who responds to the call.

The people of Chothe regard **loypi** "phython" and **əruy** "snake" as their gods. So the curry of phython and snake is their taboo particularly, while eating.

Words which are connected to sex and their functions are forbidden to be uttered in public places. Generally, people find it extremely ill-mannered to use such words. But some words, such as, **uŋa pokkə** "to give birth" and **əpum littə** "pregnant" are not regarded as taboo.

TERMS OF ADDRESS

Terms of address are proposed to express the speaker's choice of terms e.g. governing the use of first names, titles, intimate pronouns, etc. Every speaker is free to choose linguistic forms from the totality of options his language provides him. The choice of particular linguistic forms is governed by the social relationship between the speaker and hearer. The canon of choice entail planning procedures which guide the speaker in the production of, and the listener in the reception of speech.

Many languages have a distinction corresponding to the **tu-vous** (T/V) distinction in French, where grammatically there is a "singular you" **tu** (T) and a "plural you" **vous** (V) but usage requires that "you" use **vous** with individuals on certain occasions. The **T** form is sometimes described as the "familiar" form and the **V** form as the "polite" one. Other languages with a similar **T/V** distinction are Latin **(tu/vos)**, Russian **(ty/vy)**, Italian **(tu/Lei)**, German **(due/Sie)**, Swedish **(du/ni)**, and Greek **(esi/esis)**. English, itself, once had such a distinction, the **thou/you** distinction (Wardhaugh, 1986).

Language differ in the kinds of terms they use in addressing a person. Brown and Ford (1964) and Ervin-Tripp (1972) have explored terms of address in American English. In other languages, it has been found that, in addition to names, kinship terms are commonly used as terms of address, e.g. in Bengali (Das, 1964), and Hindi (Mehrotra, 1977). Some studies show that the choice of a term of address in a particular language depends on cultural values and sociological variables, as can be seen in studies by Brown and

Gilman (1960), Brown and Ford (1964), Jonz (1975), Kramer (1975), McIntire (1972), Friske (1978) and Bates and Benigni (1975). Moreover, it has also been found that the use of address terms may vary with the speaker's psychological condition, as reflected in, e.g. one's attitude towards the addressee, or one's self confidence and self respect, (Moles, 1974). Other scholars say that social changes may cause change in patterns of address, e.g. European countries (Brown and Gilman, 1960), in Sweden (Paulston, 1976 and Mitchell, 1979) and Indonesia (Wittermans, 1967).

Terms of address in Chothe are categorised by many parameters, such as age, hierarchical differences (e.g. between royalty and commoners), kinship, etc.

Age:- Age is the most important parameter for terms of address in chothe society among non relatives. In other Southeast Asian systems, a difference of even "one day" makes a person socially older (Ervin-Tripp, 1972). Age can often be a more decisive factor than social status for terms of address in Chothe. If an orderly is an older person, then he should be addressed with a senior kin term appropriate to his age. Such type of address terms are also similar in Meitei society.

Age group	**Address terms**	
Fatherly old	apu	"mother's brother"
	ətun	"uncle"
	əte/kətepa	"father's brother(elder)"
Brotherly old	kəya/əya	"elder brother"
Sisterly old	kəya/əya/kə-u-nu	"elder sister"
Motherly old	kənu/ənu	"mummy"
	əni/kətenu	"father's sister"

In addition, the middle name should follow the address term.

For instance:-

ətu
kəya/əya
kə-u-nu] + Name (middle)

The following examples are the way of address terms in the Chothe society.

(i) ətun hoŋpa "Uncle Hongpa"
(ii) kəya dimho "Elder brother Dimho"
(iii) kə-u-nu t^{h}ahoy "Elder sister Thahoi",etc.

Hierarchical differences (between royalty and commoners):- In olden times, during the monarchy, the social hierarchy was strictly adhered to royal king and queen, e.g. **əpa/kəpa reŋpa** "king" and **ənu/kənu reŋnu** "queen". **əpa/kəpa** "father" and **ənu/kənu** "mother" are the commoner terms of address. Other royal terms are not found, but nowadays, such royal terms are also lost due to the constitution of India as sovereign, socialist, secular, democratic Republic.

Kinship:- Among kins, age is not a significant factor in addressing a person. The kinship relation determines the appropriate address term. Even when a sister-in-law (elder brother's wife) is thirteen years junior in age, she should be addressed as **/kəw-u/ or /kəw-u-nu/**. According to the sociolinguistic rule it is not permitted to call her by her given name. Though a wife may be eight years older than her sister-in-law, the wife should call her sister-in-law **kəya/əya** "elder sister".

In Chothe society, a wife should not call her husband by name. She chooses the following address terms:- **məpa** "his father" **t^{h}əymo** "Are you listening to me?" and **kəjupa** "my husband". The most respect form of address is **kəjupa** to her husband. A husband calls **mənu** "his mother" to his wife. A wife calls **kəpu** to her brother-in-law and **ə-u** to her sister-in-law. **Kəpa/əpa** "father" and **kənu/ənu** "mother" are used by a wife to her father-in-law and mother-in-law respectively. A wife calls **əpu** and **əni** to her grandfather-in-law and grandmother-in-law respectively.

Name and Various Combination

In general, the surname is not used for address in Chothe society. The most common address part of a name is the middle name. Even children give only middle names when asked their name. Traditionally, the surname should precede the middle name with the final name Chothe. The last name is optional. The full name can be written in various patterns.

Examples:-

(i) Surname + Middle name + Chothe (last name)

(ii) Surname + Middle name

(iii) Middle name + Surname

(iv) Middle name + Surname + Chothe (last name)

Only pattern (i) and (iv) are used by married women. One of the above four patterns is used by men and unmarried women according to their desire.

In Chothe, profession is also indicated in the full name as given below:-

Yulung	Maipak (teacher/doctor)	Chothe
Surname	+ Middle name + (profession)	last name

Pu. is a respectable form used for man (sir) and is put before the full name, as given below:-

Pu. Yulung Maipak Chothe
(teacher/doctor)

In the same cases profession is written before the full name, for example:-

Pu. Dr. Yulung Maipak Chothe

Pi. is a respectable form used for woman (madam) and is put before the full name, as given below:-

Pi. Yulung Thahoi Chothe

The address term **/oja/** "teacher" is a very simple linguistic item which is widely accepted in Chothe society; it can be used by any speaker to any unknown addressee (in either a symmetrical or an asymmetrical relationship). By using this term, the speaker assumes an intimate relationship with the addressee.

APPENDIX I

FOLK SONG

uŋa t^{h}emnə là
child console song
"Lullaby"

(i) t^{h}a-o dekkəroŋ dekkəroŋ əntəm-pay
moon-voc. shine shine mustard-flower

pay-yəw-mo t^{h}əymu-don don-yəw-mo
flower-emph.Q.mk. berry-bud bud-emph.-Q.mk.
don-cərok-pə o-we o-we cini lom-pə
bud-big-NZ yes-SP yes-SP sugar make-NZ

lom-t^{h}əy-pə səna cek, cek
make-expert-NZ gold make make

Free translation:-

Shine, Shine, the Moon!
Has the mustard bloomed?
Has the berry-bud blossomed?
Oh! If so, well and good,
Like a sugar-maker and a goldsmith.

(ii) piŋpreəw kə-naw la-o la-o
swallow pp.-brother take-com.mk. take-com.mk.
əkin kəpa hoŋ-yəw-le
after father enter-emph.-return
dumde tuy pe-əŋ-ŋe əkin
glow-worm egg give-UNR.asp-SP after
kənu hoŋ-yəw-le səməkuŋ tuy
mother enter-emph.- return tortoise egg

pe-əŋ-ŋe
give-UNR.asp-SP

Free translation:-

Oh! swallow take my brother.
After my father comes,
I will give the egg of glow-worm.
After my mother comes,
I will give the egg of tortoise.

It is said that the elder sister sings the song when the brother cries for food, when their parents are in the field.

A SAMPLE TEXT

FOLK TALE

əmatiŋŋə	aytannu	dumdenu	səypunu
once	wild-hen	glow-worm	wild-cat

məŋəy	int^{h}um	t^{h}uy-joŋ-ŋe	məŋəy
they three	friend-make-SP		they

int^{h}um-ha	lom	ləw-se-səruy	hatəyəwk^{h}əy-yə
three-ddet	work	field-go on sugg.	but-adv.mk.

t^{h}uy-ŋəy-ha-nə	lom	t^{h}əw-we	lom-ta	bu
frield-pl-ddet-nom.	work	start-SP	work-gen	rice

lom-ta	ən-cu	lom	inpu-nə	lon-suk-kəŋ-pə
work-gen.	curry-det.	work	master-nom.	bring-out-UNR.asp-NZ

ta	li-t^{h}ak-ke	hatəwettə-cu	aytannu-ta	lom
say	say-rec.-SP	and then-det.	wild hen-gen.	work

t^{h}əw-misa-ye	hatəwettə	aytannu-nə	aytuy-nə	lom-ən
start-first-SP	and then	wild hen-nom.	egg-nom.	work-curry

lon-ne	mət^{h}əŋ-ke-nə	dumdenu-ta	lom
bring-SP	then-loc.-nom.	glow worm-gen.	work

ləw-se-ye	dumdenu-kum	ntəm-nə	lon-ən
field-go on-SP	glow worm-also	mustard-nom.	work-curry

lon-ne əsuni-nə səŋŋəypunu-ta lom ləw-se-ye
bring-SP last-non wild cat-gen. work filed-go on-SP
səŋŋəypunu-cu lom-ən əm-no-wə aytannu-ta
wild cat-det work-curry has-neg.-adv.mk. wild hen-gen.
likna yoŋ-nə aytannu-tə lak-kə
bed room search-with wild hen-acc. capture-adv.mk.
lom-ən lon-ne səŋŋəypunu-nə lom se-ke-cu
work-curry bring-SP wild cat-nom. work go on-loc.-det.
dumdenu-nə səŋŋəypunu-ke li-ye t^{h}uynu-wo
glow worm-nom. wild cat-loc. say-SP friend-voc.
iyəŋŋə-me uni nə-ləw-ta lom se-keyə aytannu
why-Q.mk. today pp-field-gen. work go on-loc wild hen
wa-no-pə-recu səŋŋəypunu-nə səŋ-ŋe aytannu-cu
come-neg.-NZ-if wild cat-nom. reply-SP wild hen-det.
ərowə wa-no-po-me mə-ləw-cu lom
how come-neg.-NZ-Q.mk. pp-field-det. work
se-yəw-k^{h}əyyə kə-ləw-cu wa-no-we
go on-emph.-finish pp-field-det come-neg.-SP
dəŋ-ni-yəw-we t^{h}uynu-wo ta wari sa-t^{h}a-kə
know-neg.-emph.-SP frield-voc. say so story talk-rec-adv.mk.
bu bək-səruy ta lom-bu lom-ən bu-sum-t^{h}a
rice eat-sugg. say so work-rice work-curry rice-pack-open
bək-ke-cu səŋŋəypunu-nə t^{h}uynu-wo tuy-mo
eat-loc.-det. wild cat-nom. frield-voc. tasty-Q.mk.
tuy-no-mo paŋ paŋ-nə bək-səruy li-yə
tasty-neg.-Q.mk. do do-adv.mk. eat-sugg. say-adv.mk.
ən-sum-t^{h}a-suk-ke-cu əru-ən əketoy-ən əke-ən
curry-pack-open-raise-loc.-dat. head-see thigh-see leg-see
ət^{h}a-ən dumdenu luŋ-keyə k^{h}ən-ne hi-cu

wing-see glow worm heart-loc. think-SP pdet-det.

kə-t^{h}uynu-ta me-nə lom-bu lom-ən lon-nə
pp-friend-gen flesh-nom. work-rice work-curry bring-adv.mk.

lon-səw-we ta mə-ta luŋ-keyə k^{h}ən-ne
bring-PER.asp.-SP say so pp-gen heart-loc. think-SP

ləw-se-su-yəw-k^{h}əyyə ə-in le-t^{h}ak-kə
field-go on-do-emph.-finish pp-home return-rec.-adv.mk.

dumdenu-nə ə-t^{h}uynu-ta ìn-ke t^{h}iŋ-ŋə
glow worm-nom. pp-frield-gen. house-loc. go-adv.mk.

ən-ke-cu aytannu əm-p^{h}uy-ni-yəw-we
look-loc.-det. wild hen live-PER.asp.-neg.-emph.-SP

ìn-keyə aytuy-ək^{h}a əm-p^{h}uy-ye aytuy-ha
house-loc. egg-one live-PER.asp-SP egg-ddet.

ayhoŋ-cəŋ-ŋə ke-ye dumdenu-nə nuŋni-ək^{h}a
cock-live-adv.mk. develop-SP glow worm-nom. day-one

loy-wa-si-ye loy-wa-keyə sinaw-wo əro-əro
roam-come-out-SP roam-come-loc. son-voc. how-how

pan-nəm-po-me ta ŋay-keyə aytante-nə
live-CON.asp-NZ-Q.mk. say so ask-loc. chicken-nom.

səŋ-ŋe nu-wo nəŋ-cu iyəŋŋə wa-po-me
reply-SP mother-voc. you-det. why come-NZ-Q.mk.

ta ŋay-keyə dumdenu-nə səŋ-ŋe kəy-rit
say so ask-loc. glow worm-nom. reply-SP I-alsso.

nə-nu-rit t^{h}uy-joŋ-t^{h}ak-ke ta wari sa-ye
pp-mother-asso. friend-make-rec.-SP say so story told-SP

nu-wo kə-nu-cu hoykeyə t^{h}iŋ-yəw-me ta
mother-voc. pp-mother-det. where go-emph.-Q.mk. say so

aytan sinaw-nə ŋay-ye dumdenu-nə saŋ-ŋe
wild hen son-nom. ask-SP glow worm-nom. reply-SP

sinaw-wo nə-nu-cu səŋŋəypunu-nə bək-t^{h}iŋ-səw-we
son-voc. pp-mother-det. wild cat-nom. eat-go-PER.asp-SP
ta wari mək^{h}Yy sa-suk-həp-pe ha-ta-recu
say so story all narrate-raise-everything-SP ddet.-gen-if
kə-nu ləmən t^{h}uy-yəŋ-ŋe ta ə-luŋ-keyə
pp-mother revenge attack-UNR.asp-SP say so pp-heart-loc.
k^{h}ən-nə aytante-nə ərowa kə-nu ləmən
think-adv.mk. chicken-nom. how pp-mother revenge
t^{h}uy-yəŋ-me ta k^{h}ən-nə k^{h}ən-nə
attack-UNR.asp-Q.mk. say so think-adv.mk. think-dv.mk.
ayhoŋpa p^{h}əw-wa-səw-we ayhoŋpə-nə ət^{h}im
cock mature-come-PER.asp-SP cock-nom. needle
t^{h}eŋku aytuy mə-ŋəy int^{h}um təməy cet-tə
hammer egg pp-pl. three very tied-adv.mk.
t^{h}uy-joŋ-səw-we nəha-cu ayhoŋpa mə-ŋəy
friend-make-PER.asp-SP oneday-det. cock pp-pl
int^{h}um-ha-ke wari sa-ye t^{h}uypa-ŋəy-yo kəy uni-cu
three-ddet.-loc. story tell-SP friend-pl-voc. I today-det.
ləmən t^{h}uy-pə sən-pi-wo ta li-keyə
revenge repaid-NZ help-HON.mk.-com.mk. say so say-loc.
mə-ŋəy int^{h}um həraw-wə ŋaypi-səw-we
pp-pl. three happy-adv.mk. agree-PER.asp-SP
ayhoŋpa-nə təməy t^{h}a-səw toŋpi-ŋəy-yo
cock-nom. very good-PER.asp friend-pl.-voc.
ha-ta-recu tutiŋ jiŋtiŋ-ke səŋŋəypunu-ta t^{h}ət-səruy ta
ddet-gen-if tomorrow night-loc. wildcat-acc. kill-sugg. say so
li-ye ha-ta-recu ət^{h}im nəŋ-nə ìnmaykot-keyə t^{h}eŋku
say-SP ddet-gen-if needle you-nom. front door-loc. harmer
nəŋ-nə ìncoykot-keyə aytuy nəŋ-nə məyp^{h}u-keyə

you-nom. back door-loc. egg you-nom. fire place-loc.
əm-mo kəy-nə kə-tʰa yap-pəŋ huŋ-ŋəŋ-ŋe
live-com.mk. I-nom. pp-wing flap-UNR.asp chirp-UNR.asp-SP
kəy-nə huŋ-keyə səŋŋəypunu-ha məypʰu-ke məy
I-nom. chirp-loc. wild cat-ddet fire place fire
sem-tʰYw-wəŋ-ŋe aytuy nəŋ-nə pokkʰay-yo ə-mit-ke
blow-start-UNR.asp-SP egg you-nom. blast-com.mk. pp-eye-loc.
ə-ut hoŋ-ŋə ìnmaykot-keyə tan-suk-kəŋ-ŋe
ash enter-adv.mk. front dooe-loc. run-raise-UNR.asp.-SP
tan-suk-ke ətʰim nəŋ-nə ə-mit-ke som-mo ha-kenə
run-raise-loc. needle you-nom. pp-eye-loc.prick-com.mk.ddet-from
ìncoykot-keyə tan-suk-kəŋ-ŋe ìncoykot-keyə
backdoor-loc. run-raise-UNR.asp.-SP backdoor-loc.
tan-suk-kəŋ-pə-keyə tʰeŋku nəŋ-nə ərukuk-keyə
run-raise-UNR.asp-NZ-loc. hammer you-nom. head-loc.
pʰilup-po ta mə ŋəy məkʰəy li-tʰak-su-wə
smash-com.mk. say so pp-pl. all say-rec.-end-adv.mk.
tʰa-səw-we tʰuyapa-wo ta li-yə mə-ŋəy
good-PER.asp.-SP friend-voc. say so say-adv.mk. pp-pl.
inli-lin toŋ-su-tʰak-səw-we tutiŋ nitak-keyə
four-together word-end-rec.-PER.asp-SP tomorrow night-loc.
ayhoŋpa-nə so-wə səŋŋəypunu-ta ìn-ke tʰiŋ-ŋə
cock-nom. start-adv.mk. wild cat-gen. house-loc go-adv.mk.
mə-ŋəy inli-lin-nə mənu ləmən tʰuy-ye
pp-pl four-together-nom. mother revange attack-SP

Free translation

Once upon a time there were three friends; a wild-cat, a wild-hen and a glow-worm. They were good friends who always shared many things and helped each other. It was time to work in the field, so they decided to help each other in their work. Since they could not work together at the time in their respective fields, they decided to work turn wise. It was decided among them that the owner of the field should provide foods for the workers while working in the field. The three frields planned to start their work, first for the wild-hen. They started working. It was time for lunch. As decided, the wild-hen had to serve her friends and for the lunch she offered them eggs. The next work was the turn of the glow-worm. They worked together and the glow-worm offered mustard leaves for them. They enjoyed the food together. The next day, they had to work for the wild-cat. The wild-cat was not having anything to make for lunch. So, the wild-cat killed the wild-hen at night, then, the wild-cat prepared it for lunch to offer their friends. In the field, the glow-worm was thinking about her friend (the wild-hen) because she was absent for the work. The glow-worm kept on asking the wild-cat about the wild-hen. But the wild-cat said nothing except blaming the wild-hen for being so selfish. As time went by, it was time for lunch and the two friends sat to eat. the glow-worm could find the body parts of her friend, the wild-hen. Then, she understood everything soon. After finishing their work she went to her friend's house to search for her where the glow-worm saw an egg lying in her friend's house but cound not find her friend.

After a few days, a chick hatched out from the egg. As time went on it turned out to be a cock. One day, the glow-worm visited the cock and told him everything about his mother how and she had been killed. The cock could not bear anymore and decided to take revenge. The cock had three friends. They were an egg, a needle and a harmmer (wooden). The cock requested them to help him to revenge his mother. They agreed happily to help him. So, they made their plan. The cock asked the egg to stay inside the furnace. He asked the needle to stay at the front door and the hammer at the back door. The cock asked the egg to explore as soon as he crowed so that the ash would go into the eyes of the wild-cat while blowing the fire. When the wild-cat ran out for help to the front door, the needle was asked to prick her eyes. Due to the severe pains the wild-cat would rush to the back door since there were no way to go. The cock requested the hammer to smash the wild-cat on her head. In this way the four friends planned to kill the wild-cat.

In the next night, the four friends came to the wild-cat's place, then, they practised their plan to kill the wild-cat. Thus the cock took revenge for his mother with the help of his friends.

APPENDIX -II

VOCABULARY

Common animals

Animals	əsa
Bear	ə-om/p^{h}uypa
Cow	si
Cat	həwtoŋ
Calf	site
Bull	sicəy
Dog	uy
Buffalo	siroy
Mitten	sirat
Tiger	əkəy
Lion	sora
Elephant	səypi
Deer	səki
Rat	əju
Pig	ok/ənoy
Sheep	lapon
Wild bear	ə-om
Monkey	əjoŋ
Horse	səkoy
Goat	əke
Fox	ləmuy
Squirrel	jurite

Common birds

Bird	əwa
Parrot	tinuwa
Crow	ak
Sparrow	usəkte
King-fisher	tuypute
Nightingale	p^{h}əyboy
Cuckoo	kokin
Vulture	ləŋtiya
Hawk	ut^{h}əwte
Goose	pəywa
Hen	aypinu
Cock	ayhoŋpa
Duck	aytok
Wild-duck	ləmaytok
Peacock	əycaŋ
Owl	məku
Bat	əbakpa

Vegetables

Cabbage	kopi
Cauliflower	kopiləy
Carrot	karot
Sweet potato	məŋkra
Potato	ərəytuy
Pepper	məsi
Green chilli	məsidikpa
Onion	ənnim
Garlic	əyp^{h}uyri
Tomato	məntot^{h}uypa
Ginger	əyt^{h}iŋ
Bean	əbe
Soyabean	basəw

Pumkin	əmay
Mustard leaf	əntəm əbu
Brinjal	mənto
Pea	məŋkən
Gourd	um
Lady's finger	b^{h}elendari

Fruits

Orange	komla
Lemon	t^{h}əyt^{h}uy
Apple	t^{h}əytup
Papaya	əwasəkma
Berry	t^{h}əymura
Mango	t^{h}əyhay
Plum	t^{h}əyk^{h}a
Guava	bərəytun
Banana	əmot
Pear	naspati
Pomegranate	kəpot^{h}əy
Olive	corp^{h}on

Common Insects

Ant	səŋŋi
Mosquito	təŋt^{h}an
Fly	t^{h}əw
Bee	t^{h}əwhuy
Black bee	huymu
Spider	moyməraŋcaŋ
Butterfly	p^{h}urup
Dragonfly	ceklaŋ
Glow-worm	dumde
Moth	p^{h}urupte
Locust	haw
Grass hopper	koŋkrik
Beetle	ekmuy
Burning beetle	kəŋkuycep
Crockroach	kəŋkrawpi
Bug	əsat
Louse	lik
White ant	ləyt^{h}a
Frog	uytok

Kinship-terms And Forms of Address

Father	əpa
Mother	ənu
Father's brother (younger)	kətun
Father's brother (elder)	kəte
Mother's brother	kəpute
Mother's sister	kətenu
Brother(e)	kə-u-pa
Brother(y)	kanawpa
Sister(e)	kə-u-nu
Sister(y)	kəsəynu
Mother in law	kəni
Father in law	kəpu/kərəŋ
Sister in law	kə-u
Cousin(brother)	sellebay
Brother in law	kəbay
Aunt	kənute/ kətenu

Common diseases

Common cold	əsik
Fever	ətun
Influenza	ətunt^{h}əwwa
Typhoid	suŋtu

Diarrhea	t^{h}uywa-əna
Head ach	luna
Cholera	suŋt^{h}uy
vomitting	lupa
hospital	əna-ənna-in
tuberculosis	huwa-əna
doctor	ət^{h}im
localphysician	ət^{h}impu
midwife	t^{h}impi
nurse	ənasipaen
operation	cəmnawatta
swelling	pumt^{h}əwwa
itching	əja
leprocy	ləyci-oyya
diabetis	tuyt^{h}iŋŋa
blind	mitcowa
deaf	nukuyset
dump	toŋsukno
lame	ketikpa
handicap	soynəypa
medicine	ləw-əy

Name of the Month

Month	t^{h}a
Sunday	soyhakni
Monday	əthəwni
Tuesday	ləysemni
Wednesday	insakni
Thursday	əhayni
Friday	tuyni
Saturday	əsuni
Today	uni
Yesterday	əjan
Tomorrow	tutiŋ
Day before Yesterday	ətip
Last month	əmət^{h}a
Next month	wa-əmmət^{h}a
Last year	əməkum
Next year	waəmməkum

Common goods of daily use

Grass	t^{h}iŋna
Glass	likok
Tumbler	wansaŋ
Plate	b^{h}u
Chair	lahaŋ
Bed	kukaŋ
Box	t^{h}im-t^{h}uy
Almirah	almira
Cloth	pun
Shirt	liŋlut
Trouser	k^{h}oŋkraw
Water	tuy
Air	t^{h}iraŋ
Paper	nà
Ink	muk
Book	əbay
Pen	kolom
Pencil	pencil
Shoe	kekok
Shocks	kemoca
Lock	so
Key	socəy
Door	kot
Window	kotte
Fire	sayməy
Firewood	səŋlŋt^{h}iŋ
Bucket	tuyronna
Pot	be
Ladle	hatəy

Light	əwaypa	Sugar	ət^{h}um
Woollen cloth	samuypun	Curry	ən
Health	pum	Cow dung	si-ek
Pillar	əco	Coe-shed	si-kum
Quilt	punhu	Court yard	tumay
Wall	ìnbəŋ	Verenda	məŋkuy
Thatch	ləŋi	Grainery store	səŋpəŋ
Roof	ìncuŋ	Kitchen	bukəmnain
Song	la	Mat	p^{h}əy
Rice	bu	Bed sheet	punp^{h}a
Liquor	ju	Picture	ləyhu
Bread	butoy	Bamboo	əru
Egg	aytuy	Reed	peroŋ
Milk	səŋkom/	Sliced bamboo	ta
	nukutuy	Basket	tay
Meat	me	Fish	tuyrik
Flesh	metək	Oil	ət^{h}əw
Pork	okme	Mustard oil	əntəm t^{h}əw
Beef	sime	Market	əp^{h}əy/kəyt^{h}i
Tea	ca	Road	ləmpi
Coffee	cop^{h}i	Bell	kənta
Chicken	ayme	Sun	ni
Mosquito net	həŋəy	Moon	kərosompa/t^{h}a
Mattress	muypek	Earth	simləy
Pillow	mun	Star	əysi
Cigarette	t^{h}əkna	New moon	t^{h}at^{h}əy
Knife	cəmte	Full moon	t^{h}at^{h}uy/t^{h}asu
Dagger	lamcəm	New year	kumt^{h}əy
Sword	cəməsəypa	Summer	asawt^{h}a
Axe	ərəy	Winter	p^{h}əybi
Spear	səy	Rainy season	suypitin
Shield	p^{h}o	Hill	muyron
Gun	əhutsoŋ	River	tuywa
Bottle	yuhom	Pond	tuykuk
Salt	ci	Tree	t^{h}iŋlok/t^{h}iŋ

Ocean	tuyrikuk
Lake	tuyrijay
Wave	tuysəyron
Current	tuytan
River	tuywa
Stream	tuydaŋ
Dry	əcay
Sky	əwansaŋ
East	nisukna
West	nitak
South	tʰaŋtiŋ
North	saktiŋ

Colours

Colour	əsəŋna
White	əŋəwpə
Black	əhaŋ
Red	əsən
Green	ədik
Sky-blue	dikcoŋpə
Yellow	sənləwpə
Purple	sənconpə
Grey	ŋəwpuypə

Pronouns

I	kəy
We	kəni/əni
You(sg./pl.)	nəŋ
He/she	əmo
They	məŋŋəy
Me	kəyta
My	kəta
Yours	nəta
His/her	məta
Him/her	əmota
Their	məŋəyta
Them	mənita
Our	ənita

Question words

Who	ətu
What	ì
Which	iropa
Where	hoyke
When	itikkə
How	irowa/ərowa
Why	iyəŋŋə

Parts of the Body

Hair	tonsəm
Eye	məysəy/mit
Ear	nukuy
Nose	natuŋ
Chick	betak
Lip	nəy
Face	soymay/may
Head	lu/tʰiŋlu
Teeth	ha
Tongue	bərəy
Gum	hakuŋ
Neck	hoŋ
Chest	taŋ
Breast	nuku/pumli
Belly	won
Hand	cəŋban
Palm	kʰutpʰa
Thump	kʰutpi
Iron finger	kʰutjay
Small finger	kʰutte
Waist	koŋ
Wrist	kʰuttoŋ
Elbow	əkʰutniŋ

Shoulder	liŋkəw
Stomach	wonpi
Heart	luŋ
Lungs	luŋhe
Hip	dop
Knee	hokpu
Leg	ke
Heel	ketoŋ
Toe(s)	keripay
Skin	unkoy
Bone	səru
Blood	ət^{h}i
Body hair	mùy
Nail	tiŋ
Mouth	muyhəw/muy
Brain	lut^{h}uk
Intestine	əri
Liver	əsəra
Naval	ray
Eye-lash	mit-muy
Eye-brow	mitkuy
Eye-lid	mithəw
Chin	rəha
Eye-ball	mitte
Throat	loyto
Thigh	toy
Back bone	əjay səru
Nerve	pəjəŋ
Forehead	cəypaŋ
Trunk	əjaŋ

Numerals

One	ək^{h}a
Two	əni
Three	int^{h}um
Four	inli
Five	rəŋa
Six	əruk
Seven	səri
Eight	əret
Nine	əku
Ten	əsom
Eleven	əsomək^{h}a
Twelve	əsoməni
Thirteen	əsomint^{h}um
Fourteen	əsominli
Fifteen	əsomrəŋa
Sixteen	əsoməruk
Seventeen	əsomsəri
Eighteen	əsoməret
Nineteen	əsoməku
Twenty	somni
Twentyone	somniək^{h}a
Twentytwo	somniəni
Twentythree	somniint^{h}um
Twentyfour	somniinli
Twentyfive	somnirəŋa
Twentysix	somniəruk
Twentyseven	somnisəri
Twentyeight	somniəret
Twentynine	somniəku
Thirty	somt^{h}um
Thirtyone	somt^{h}umək^{h}a
Thirtytwo	somt^{h}uməni
Thirtythree	somt^{h}umint^{h}um
Thirrtyfour	somt^{h}uminli
Thirtyfive	somt^{h}umrəŋa
Thirtysix	somt^{h}uməruk
Thirtyseven	somt^{h}umsəri
Thirtyeight	somt^{h}uməret
Thirtynine	somt^{h}uməku
Forty	somli

Fortyone	somliəkʰa	Seventyseven	somsərisəri
Fortytwo	somliəni	Seventyeight	somsəriəret
Fortythree	somliintʰum	Seventynine	somsəriəku
Fortyfour	somliinli	Eighty	somret
Fortyfive	somlirəŋa	Eightyone	somretəkʰa
Fortysix	somliəruk	Eightytwo	somretəni
Fortyseven	somlisəri	Eightythree	somretintʰum
Fortyeight	somliəret	Eightyfour	somretinli
Fortynine	somliəku	Eightyfive	somretrəŋa
Fifty	somŋa	Eightysix	somretəruk
Fiftyone	somŋaəkʰa	Eightyseven	somretsəri
Fiftytwo	somŋaəni	Eightyeight	somretəret
Fiftythree	somŋaintʰum	Eightynine	somretəku
Fiftyfour	somŋainli	Ninety	somku
Fiftyfive	somŋarəŋa	Ninetyone	somkuəkʰa
Fiftysix	somŋaəruk	Ninetytwo	somkuəni
Fiftyseven	somŋasəri	Ninetythree	somkuintʰum
Fiftyeight	somŋaəret	Ninetyfour	somkuinli
Fiftynine	somŋaəku	Ninetyfive	somkurəŋa
Sixty	somruk	Ninetysix	somkuəruk
Sixtyone	somrukəkʰa	Ninetyseven	somkusəri
Sixtytwo	somrukəni	Ninetyeight	somkuəret
Sixtythree	somrukintʰum	Ninetynine	somkuəku
Sixtyfour	somrukinli	One hundred	lihakʰa
Sixtyfive	somrukrəŋa	Two hundred	lihani
Sixtysix	somrukəruk	Three hundred	lihatʰum
Sixtyseven	somruksəri	Four hundred	lihali
Sixtyeight	somrukəret	Five hundred	lihaŋa
Sixtynine	somrukəku	Six hundred	liharuk
Seventy	somsəri	Seven hundred	lihasəri
Seventyone	somsəriəkʰa	Eight hundred	liharet
Seventytwo	somsəriəni	Nine hundred	lihaku
Seventythree	somsəriintʰum	Ten hundred	lihasom
Seventyfour	somsəriinli	Twenty hundred	lihasomni
Seventyfive	somsərirəŋa	Thirty hundred	lihasomtʰum
Seventysix	somsəriəruk	Forty hundred	lihasomli

Fifty hundred	lihasomŋa
Sixty hundred	lihasomruk
Seventy hundred	lihasomsəri
Eighty hundred	lihasomret
Ninety hundred	lihasomku
Thousand	lisiŋ

Ordinal numbers

First	misapə
Second	ənisupə
Third	int^{h}umsupə
Fourth	inlisupə
Fifth	rəŋasupə
Sixth	əruksupə
Seventh	sərisupə
Eighth	əretsupə
Nineth	əkusupə
Tenth	əsomsupə

APPENDIX-III

Additional Vocabulary

English	Word
Able	ne
Accuse	əjuyəran
Ache	əy
Admit	lutpipə
Again	leya
After	ətakke
Ago	əmatiŋ
Age	kùm
Agree	əŋay
Air	tʰiraŋ
All	ətəmpə
Alone	ətʰəncək
Always	əpʰa cəŋonna
Amend	tʰapiya
And	əkʰakum
Anger	luŋsapə
Annex	lahoŋpə
Answer	səŋŋa
Appetite	wontama
Apple	tʰəytup
Appoint	ŋəmhoŋŋa
Arrive	tuŋpə
Arrow	tʰəyru
Ash	ə-ut
Ask	loŋŋaypə
Bad	tʰarəwpə
Bake	tʰəwwa
Bald	ludepə
Balk	əyetpə
Ban	ŋayrəwpə
Bank	tuywahəw
Bark	tʰiŋkoy
Bath	təkbuywa
Beak	əmuy
Beat	huk
Become	wa-əmpə
Before	əmake
Begin	tʰəwpə
Below	ətʰuy
Between	əkarak
Big	rok
Bind	hup
Bite	əypə
Bitter	kʰəcakpə
Blind	maysəycopə
Blow	jap
Blunt	popnopə
Blur	əjiktʰiŋləwpə
Boat	kuŋ
Body	pumpaŋ
Boil(v)	pʰuypiya
Boil(n)	pʰuya
Bold	ərat-əraŋ
Box	tʰim
Bow	pʰəydaŋ
Boy	əpate
Bracelet	koy
Branch	əbak
Break	kuypə
Breathe	tʰuktʰaytʰaypə
Breeze	tʰiraŋ
Bright	deropə
Bring	lonwapə

Bubble	səw
Bud	əmum
Bunch	əcom
Burn	kaŋpə
Busy	ciya/cipə
Cage	əsa-əŋakuń
Calculate	tepə
Calm	daycomma
Cane	ətiŋ
Care	siŋetpə
Carry	coywapə
Catch	mənpə
Chance	təncap^{h}əpə
Change	t^{h}oŋsakpə
Chapter	əkəm
Charcoal	məyek
Charm	əhoypə
Chase	juyt^{h}akpə
Cheap	ətompə
Cheat	əmuyt^{h}əypə
Cheese	nukutuyət^{h}əw
Choice	t^{h}əŋt^{h}əwpə
Claw	əsaəŋaketiŋ
Clear	t^{h}iŋkripə
Climb	kəyhəŋpə
Close	humpə
Cloud	sump^{h}ay
Coarse	loypə
Cold	day
Collide	suhoŋt^{h}akpə
Combine	tuyhoŋpə
Come	wa
Commerce	ləyuyletik
Compare	caŋənt^{h}akpə
Condition	ciləm
Consider	wəysipə
Console	t^{h}emhoŋpə
Conspire	əsuŋtoŋwaysipə
Continue	ət^{h}uyt^{h}iŋjuypə
Cook	bukəmpə
Cotton	lacon
Country	mirəm
Courage	əraŋpə
Coward	jəm
Crab	ay
Cradle	nəwhuŋna
Cruel	luŋsit^{h}əynopə
Curtain	punduŋŋa
Cut	tən
Curry	ən
Dagger	somnacəm
Damage	maŋpipə
Dance	lam
Danger	ə-oypə
Dark	ət^{h}impə
Dawn	həyiŋdəŋ
Day	luŋni
Deaf	kuysetpə
Dear	liŋləypə
Debt	ləydon
Decide	toŋŋir
Delay	taypə
Demand	tàypə
Depend	ət^{h}uydoypə
Die	t^{h}i
Difficult	lupə
Dig	cəw
Disease	ərəyna
Distance	ləmrapə
Divide	səmpə
Divorce	t^{h}ənt^{h}akpə

Do	e
Door	kot
Dream	məŋ
Dress	buyrəy
Drink	in
Drive	com
Dust	up^{h}un
Duty	əŋəm
Each	ək^{h}arit
Eager	lanuma
Eat	bək
Eel fish	ŋaruy
Elder	ulincəŋpə
Empty	əruksa
End	əsupə
Enemy	əndoyəndapə
Enough	əhopə
Enter	hoŋ
Equal	əŋk^{h}apə
Escape	naysukpə
Event	t^{h}əwt^{h}uk
Evil	t^{h}arəwpə
Express	lisukpə
Extinguish	mitpə
Fail	nenopə
Fall	tuypə
Famine	butaŋpə
Far	ləmlapə
Fat	sapə
Fear	ətipə
Feed	bəkpipə
Field	ləwmuy
Fight	p^{h}itt^{h}akpə
Find	tukpə
Finish	əsupə
Flame	məybrəy
Flat	p^{h}əyjoy
Float	taw
Floor	simləy
Fly	yuŋ/juŋ
Foam	tuyp^{h}uy
Fog	sump^{h}ay
Fold	t^{h}ep
Food	səkcak
Fool	pəŋ
Forget	mək
Fort	cipənk^{h}a
Freeze	p^{h}əmhoŋpə
Fresh	liŋdikdikpə
Friend	toŋpi
Frog	uytok
Fun	ərimpə
Future	ətakta
Gale	t^{h}iraŋp^{h}əybu
Game	lak^{h}a
Garden	jəwkun
Gate	kont^{h}oŋ
Gentle	luŋcəlhoypə
Get	p^{h}a
Gift	liŋləyya-pet^{h}akpəpot
Girl	numəyte
Give	pe
Gland	t^{h}əyt^{h}əwpə
Go	t^{h}iŋ
God	ləyhu
Gold	sana
Grave	t^{h}anp^{h}əm
Great	əlok-əsəy
Group	mirim

Habbit	ətʰəy	Invent	coysukpə
Half	əhuy	It	hina
Hammer	cəmsunaətʰiŋləŋ	Ink	muk
Hang	tʰoy	Jar	luŋjube
Hard	kən	Jaleous	ənəypə
Harm	maŋnaŋəm	Journey	ləmtʰiŋpə
Husk	suway	Joy	ərimpə
Hate	əndoyəndapə	Juice	ətuy
Hear	tʰəy/ŋay	Jump	com
Heat	məysa	Jute	əntʰuyluy
Heavy	rit	Joke	əjayəsim
Here	hinake	Jacket	liŋlutəkəwpə
Hide	tʰup	Keep	sipə
Hit	huk	Kick	təpənpə
Host	ìnpu	Kill	tʰət
Hoist	kəytʰəwpə	King	əreŋ
Hole	əhuy	Kiss	cup
Home	ìn	Know	dəŋ
Honest	luŋtʰiŋpə	Knight	ərok-əsəy
Hope	luŋniŋ	Ladle	hetəy
Horn	əki	Large	əroy
Hot	əsapə	Late	təy
Hour	puŋsiŋ	Lie	mutʰəy
Humble	haycapə	Laugh	nuy
Hurt	toŋpə	Leaf	nukuy
Ice	ə-uy	Leak	səy
Idle	ludoypə	Learn	cu
Ill	nenopə	Left(N)	woy
In	əsuŋta	Length	əduŋ
Incline	lonhəŋpə	Lick	lik
Increase	hehəŋpə	Life	əpunsi
Infinite	əsuəroməmləwpə	Like	di
Inquire	johoŋpə	Line	lə-i
Insult	əjəkpə	Liquid	ətuy
Iron	ətʰi	Little	əsin

Look	ən	Origin	ət^{h}əwna
Loose	kum	Other	ədəŋ
Love	liŋləy	Paddy	saŋ
Low	nim	Page	nərəŋ
Mad	wet	Pedal	səroy
Make	sa	Pet	ŋuy
Man	əpa	Picture	ləyhu
Marriage	təyt^{h}apə	Piece	əprep
Meal	bubək	Place	əmun
Medicine	ləw	Play	lak^{h}apə
Meet	tuŋt^{h}ak	Plenty	don
Modest	nəwpənekpə	Poor	sarapə
Mole	p^{h}əyməron	Pour	bun
Morning	ətuk	Praise	toŋt^{h}iŋna
Mother	kənu	Prize	jaymən
Mourn	hoyya	Proud	lokcokpə
Mud	juntok	Price	əmən
More	heyə	Pull	kəypə
Nest	əkun	Pure	ət^{h}iŋpə
Net	caŋ	Put	si
New	ət^{h}əy	Quench	məkpinepə
News	t^{h}əypiyatoŋ	Quiet	ənjon
Next	ətak	Quick	ənot
Nice	ənjon	Quote	təysuk
Night	jintiŋ	Race	əjat
Now	ətunna	Rainbow	luypit^{h}əw
Nephew	kətukəmak	Rain	lu
Name	əmiŋ	Read	ənno
No	ənopə	Reap	pot
Nor	ənohəppə	Reduce	lejuŋ
Oath	sərəw	Repeat	leya
Old	taypu	Rest	soyha
On	əcuŋ	Return	lewa
Or	hənanore	Rich	əcoŋ
Open	hoŋpə	Riddle	jaysesumsepə

Ride	cuŋ
Ring	kʰusəbik
Ripe	min
Rise	tʰəw
Road	ləmpi
Rock	əruŋ
Roof	ìncuŋ
Root	əjuŋ
Rotten	ətʰu-ənəw
Round	kuy
Rub	nuysuk
Run	tan
Rich	əcoŋ
Roar	lam
Report	putəmma
Revenge	məruŋsuypə
Reserve	həyyasipə
Rim	təmmə
Rear	nuŋtiŋ
Review	leyaənhoŋpə
Reality	ətʰiŋpə
Realize	dəŋwapə
Release	tʰajokpə
Sad	woy
Saline	ci-əypə
Sale	juypə
Sand	ləyŋuy
Save	kənpipə
See	li
Say	li
Scold	luŋsa
Score	cəy
Shout	əw
Seed	əmu
Seek	joŋ
Select	tʰəŋ
Send	tʰatʰiŋ
Shadow	tʰəway
Shield	pʰo
Shut	kəypə
Sit	oŋ
Sleep	jay
Slow	sum
Small	sin
Smile	nuyrim
Snow	ə-uy
So	hanacəŋŋə
Soft	nem
Some	ətəy
Song	la
Soon	ənottə
Sorrow	ə-oypə
Sound	ətra
Soup	əntuy
Space	tʰaŋwan
Spade	ətu
Speak	toŋlipə
Spit	cisakpə
Spoon	həttəy
Stand	ŋi
Strainer	bubitay
Starve	buhəypə
Steal	ilu
Step	kehap
Stop	ŋi
Straw	cipʰo
Surface	simləycuŋ
Swim	tuyjakka
Tail	əməy

Tailor	puntupə	Turn	lesuk
Take	la	Twin	əp^{h}i
Tall	əsəy	Twist	nok
Tame	əŋuy	Ugly	me-əsi
Teach	cupipə	Unite	tuypə
Tear(N)	mittuy	Vain	ərim
Tear(V)	t^{h}e	Vast	əlokpə
Tease	loynapə	Very	təməy
Test	t^{h}əymotaənpə	Vibrate	ənotanokpə
Thank	domma	Village	hu
Thatch	ləŋi	Voice	əroy
There	hake	Wage	əman
Thick	sa	Wait	hak
Thief	lu/inlu	Wake	int^{h}əwpə
Thin	toy	Walk	t^{h}iŋ
Thorn	əriŋ	Want	di
Thought	luŋlaŋ	War	lay
Thread	la	Warm	lum
Threat	ətipi	Wash	si
Throw	deŋ/jun	Wave	tuysərun
Thunder	luri	Wax	əca
Tie	suy	Wealth	ləy
Time	əp^{h}a	Wet	ci
Tire	t^{h}ajuŋ	Wheat	gehu
Tyre	tayar	Wheel	cəkka
Today	uni	Wide	pek
Top	əlepay	Win	t^{h}uy
Tortoise	sənəkuŋ	Wing	ət^{h}a
Touch	toŋ	Witch	doyəyt^{h}əynu
Town	məraŋjay	Woman	numəy
Toy	uŋaləknɔ	Word	toŋlo
Trap	caŋ	Write	hut
Tremble	ətiyanokpə	Wrong	suy
True	ədik	Year	kum
Try	caŋ-ənpə	Yes	oy

Young	nawpoŋ
Youth	luyt^{h}əy
Zeal	luŋluttanipə
Zero	jero
Zoo	əsasinakun

BIBLIOGRAPHY

Adam, Valerie,1973. *An Introduction to Mordern English Word-Formation*. Longman Group Limited.

Anderson, Stephen, 1974. *The Organization of Phonology*. Academic Press, INC, (London) LTD.

Bauer, Laurie, 1983. *English Word-Formation*. Cambridge University Press. Cambridge, English.

Bhaskarao, Pari, 1972. *Practical Phonetics Part I* CASL. University of Poona.

Bhat, D.n.s. 1978. *Pronominalisation* . Poona Decan College.

Bhat S.N.S. and M.S. Ningomba, 1995. *Manipuri Grammar*. CIIL Mysore.

Bloomfield, D. 1935. *Language*. Allen and Unwin.

Catfort, J.C. 1988. *A Practical: Introduction to Phonetics*. Oxford University Press.

Chomsky, N. 1965. *Aspects of Theory of Syntax*. MIT Press Cambridge.

Clack John, and Yallop, 1990. *An Introduction to Phonetics and Phonology*. Cambridge.

Comrie, Bernand, 1985a. *Tense*. Cambridge University Press

Deutsch, Andre, 1959. *Mordern Linguistics*. © Simeon Potter.

Daniel, Jones, 1922 (Rep.1997). *An Outline of English Phonetics*. Cambridge University Press.

Das, Sisir Kumar, 1968. *Form of Address and Terms of Reference of Bengali*. Anthropological Linguistics.

Devi Nameirakpam Pramodini, 1989. *Social Grammar of Meiteilon*. (Unpublished Doctoral Desertation) Manipur University.

Dutta Baruah, P.N. and Bapui, V.L.T. 1996. *Hmar Grammar*. CIIL Mysore.

Fiske, Shirley, 1978. *Rules of Address: Navajo Women in Los Angeles*. Journal of Anthropological Research.

Francis, P. and Dinnen, S.J. 1967. *An Introduction to General Linguistics*. Halt, Rinehart and Winston INC.

Francis, W. N. 1983. *Dialectology: An Introduction*. Longman Group Limited. Longman House, England.

Giridhar P.P. 1994. *Mao Naga Grammar*. CIIL, Mysore.

Grierson, G.A. 1904. *Linguistic Survey of India Vol.3 Part III*. Culcutta Reprinted 1967, Motilal Banarasidas, Delhi.

Gurubasave Gowda, K.S. 1975. 1975. *Ao Grammar*. CIIL, Mysore.

Greenberg, J.H. 1964. *Universal of Language* 2nd Edition. Cambridge Mass MIT Press.

Hass, M.R. 1995. *Interlingual Word Taboo*. American Anthropological.

Hale, A. 1982. *Research on Tibeto-Burman Languages*. Trends in Linguistics, Mouton.

Hawkins, Peter. 1984 (Rep.1995). *Introducing Phonology*. Routledge II New Fetler Lane, London.

Hockett, Charles F. 1958. A Course In Mordern Linguistics. New York, U.S.A.. The Macmillan Co.

Hall Robert A. 1969. *Introduction to Linguistics*. Chilton Company, Motilal Banarasidas Delhi.

Jespersen, O. 1917. *Negation in English and Other Language*. Selected Writing, London.

Kachru Yamuna, 1980. *Aspects of Hindi Grammar*. Ramesh Jain Manohar Publications.Darya Ganj, New Delhi.

Katz and Paul. 1964 *An Integrated Theory Of Linguistic Descriptions*. Cambridge: MIT Press.

Lass, Roger. 1984. *Phonology. An Introduction to Basic Concepts*. Cambridge University Press.

Lyons John, 1968. *An Introduction to Theoretical Linguistics*. Cambridge University.

Matisoff, James A. 1973. *The Grammar of Lahu*. University of California Press, Berkeley.

Mathews, PH. 1991. *Morphology.* Cambridge University Press.

Modhubala, P. 1979. *Manipuri Grammar*. Unpublished Ph.D. Dissertation Deccan College. Poona.

Ramaswami, N. 1999. *Common Linguistic Features in Indian Languages: Phonetics*. CIIL, Mysore.

Robins, R.H. 1964. *General Linguistics*. An Introducing Survey. Longman Group Ltd.

Shing Ch. Yashawanta. 2000. *Manipuri Grammar*. Rajesh Publications New Delhi.

————2002. *Tarao Grammar*. Akansha Publishing House New Delhi.

Shing H. Brojen. 2000. *A Descriptive Grammar of Chothe*. Unpublished Ph.D. Thesis. Manipur University.

Shing, Kh. Loken. 1997. *Word-Formation in Kuki-Chin Group*. Unpublished Ph. D. Thesis. Manipur University.

Shing, M. Shamungou. 1995. *A. Descriptive Grammar of Aimol.* Unpublished Ph. D. Thesis. Manipur University

Standhope, Y. 1986. *Chothe Ngei Athouna Yongna*. Imphal.

Shobhana, L.C. 1997. *A Grammar of Meitei*. Mouton de Gruyter, Berlin, New York.

Syal, P. and Jindal D.V. 1998. *An Introduction to Linguistics. Language, Grammar and Semantics*. Prentice-Hall of India Private Limited. New Delhi.

Thoudam, P.C. 1991. ANM. Enterprises. *TDC. Remedial Manipuri.* Singjamei, Imphal.

Wardhaugh, Ronald. 1986. *An Introduction to Sociolinguistics*. Basil Blackwell Ltd., New York..

Yule Geoge, 1985. *The Study of Language*. Cambridge University Press.

Zandvoort, R.W. 1972(Reprinted). *A Hand Book of English Grammar*. ELBS and Longman Group Ltd.

Zograph, G.A. 1980. *Language of South Asia. A guide*. London Longman.